Wings for
My Flight

UNM
GALLUP

Zollinger Library

WINGS FOR MY FLIGHT

The Peregrine Falcons of Chimney Rock

Marcy Cottrell Houle

UPDATED EDITION

University of New Mexico Press · Albuquerque

Many of the designations used by manufacturers and sellers to distinguish their products are claimed as trademarks. Where those designations appear in this book and Addison-Wesley was aware of a trademark claim, the designations have been printed in initial capital letters (e.g., Styrofoam).

© 1991 by Marcy Cottrell Houle
All rights reserved.
First University of New Mexico Press edition published 2014 by arrangement with the author

Printed in the United States of America
19 18 17 16 15 14   1 2 3 4 5 6

LIBRARY OF CONGRESS CATALOGING-IN-PUBLICATION DATA
Houle, Marcy Cottrell, 1953–
  Wings for my flight : the peregrine falcons of Chimney Rock / Marcy Cottrell Houle. — First University of New Mexico Press edition 2014.
     pages cm
  "Originally published in hardcover by Addison-Wesley, 1991."
  Summary: "The story of the near-extinction of the American Peregrine Falcon, and the fight to save it against tremendous odds"— Provided by publisher.
  ISBN 978-0-8263-5434-1 (pbk. : alk. paper) — ISBN 978-0-8263-5435-8 (electronic)
   1. Peregrine falcon—Colorado—Chimney Rock (Archuleta County) 2. Houle, Marcy Cottrell, 1953– I. Title.
  QL696.F34H68 2014
  598.9'60978832—dc23

                              2013027324

All photos courtesy of the author.

To Dr. James Enderson,
who instilled in all his students the love of the peregrine,
and to John,
who came to share it with me.

FOREWORD

*T*WELVE YEARS AGO, in the autumn, an attractive young woman came to my front door in Jackson Hole and introduced herself. As we talked, she told me about her summer of watching and studying a peregrine falcon's nest in a national forest in southern Colorado. She was very worried about the future of these remarkable birds, because of roads and potential intensive development too near their nesting site.

I remember her saying, "I don't care about me or my job. What really matters is those birds."

Marcy Cottrell went back to that job for three more seasons, and here is her story. The reader may find it hardly believable, but I know it is true.

Marcy found misunderstanding, anger, and violence. She also found friendship and cooperation. And this is a love story too.

Woven through this narrative is rich information—first-hand knowledge, impressive word pictures—about one of the endangered species of our world.

Now we can all hope, with Marcy, that peregrines may again use that perfect place, the cliff at Chimney Rock—for the enrichment of us all.

MARGARET E. MURIE

PUBLISHER'S NOTE

*T*HE FOLLOWING STORY recounts the author's experiences while protecting and studying nesting peregrine falcons at Chimney Rock, Colorado. Her involvement with the Chimney Rock study extended from 1975 to 1978. Most of what is told here occurred during the first nesting season, but some events from later years have been treated as though they took place in the first year. Most personal and place names have been changed to avoid any unintended embarrassment to the participants. All facts about the peregrines are documented, but conversations in the book reflect the memory of the author. With these few qualifications, what follows accurately recounts an especially dramatic example of the ongoing worldwide fight to protect animals and preserve the variety of life with which our planet is endowed.

Sky, be my depth;
Wind, be my width and my height;
World, my heart's span:
Loneliness, wings for my flight.

—*Leonora Speyer*
from "Measure Me, Sky"

PREFACE
TO THE UPDATED EDITION

*A*T FIRST, THE silhouette moving quickly in the distance did not register as anything out of the ordinary. I took it for the back-lit form of a hawk. We had plenty of redtails, ospreys, and kestrels on our Oregon island farm, and the sight of them soaring always gave me pleasure. But as this bird neared, something about its sleek, dark outline, its speed and sheer exuberance, seemed different.

Suddenly I stopped, unable to breathe. As the image flew overhead, I could see the smooth blue feathers, the arced, pointed wings, and the jet-black head of a peregrine falcon.

The significance of its presence was staggering for a moment. Spying me, the peregrine dipped down, then shot skyward with such power as if expelled by a rocket blast. The creature's beauty, agility, and grace had never failed to fill me with awe. Yet this time, the emotion was even more profound: I had been taken full circle. I was watching a wild peregrine falcon flying freely in a field—*outside my own front door.*

Sweeter still, the sight was the culmination of a success story—two stories actually—about a species and a place. Not so very long ago, success for either one had seemed not only improbable, but impossible.

I knew, too well, how close we came to losing both forever.

Less than forty years ago, the chance that the American peregrine falcon—the fastest-moving species in the world—would even more catastrophic. Chimney Rock, and the thousands of acres surrounding it, was slated for coal extraction.

The formidable goals of preserving a spiritual homeland in the face of such grand development and extraction plans, as well as rescuing a species of bird on the cusp of extinction, seemed, by all counts, unattainable. Yet four things happened in the mid-1970s whose outcome no one could have then predicted. Four things made all the difference and, in time, transformed the futures of both:

1. In 1972, DDT was banned for most uses in the United States.
2. The Endangered Species Act, the nation's most visionary conservation law, was enacted by Congress in 1973. This vital legislation became the crucial vehicle leading to success for the peregrine falcon. Coming just in time, the Endangered Species Act mandated the formation and funding of recovery plans for endangered species and brought together teams of the best minds to design strategies for averting extinction. Without the Endangered Species Act and the funding it provided, peregrine recovery teams and plans, as well as any significant measure of propagation and release of captive falcons, would not have been possible.
3. In 1974, the Peregrine Fund, the Colorado Division of Wildlife, and scientists such as James Enderson, Tom Cade, and Jerry Craig, among many others, saw the first glimmers of hope for the peregrine when they began successfully releasing captively raised peregrines back into the wild. The dream to "restock" dwindling and absent populations throughout North America by freeing birds raised in captivity was to become a viable and effective recovery method. From 1974 to 1994, over six thousand captively raised peregrines were released into the wild.
4. Under the Endangered Species Act, the preservation of an endangered species takes priority over other potential land uses. When peregrine falcons were found to be nesting at Chimney

Rock, the grand-scale development of the area was placed on hold. For fifteen years, all expansion plans stopped, and coal was not leased. This imposed hiatus provided time for a new vision of the real values of the Chimney Rock archaeological area to formulate and find momentum.

The commitment to saving the peregrine was a joint effort involving thousands of scientists, falconers, and volunteers. Working together, their single-minded devotion became the greatest, most cooperative, and most comprehensive undertaking to rescue an endangered species ever attempted. Because of these dedicated efforts, the peregrine began, slowly at first, to increase in number. The "turnaround" for the falcons began in 1985; by 1994, over a thousand pairs of peregrines were again nesting in North America. By 1998, peregrine falcons had reclaimed most of their historical territories and their reproduction had once again returned to normal. With such a degree of success, in 1999 peregrine falcons were removed from the federal list of endangered species—a magnificent achievement.

Today, numbers of peregrine falcons are still continuing to increase. In their book *Peregrine Falcons of the World*, falcon biologists Clayton White, Tom Cade, and James Enderson[*] estimate that 3,100 pairs of *Falco peregrinus anatum* resided in North America in 2012—a number unthinkable in 1975, when fewer than twelve pairs of peregrines were known in the Rockies, and fewer than one hundred in the contiguous United States!

A second success story also took place in 2012. After years of grassroots activism by citizen groups, historic and archaeological preservation alliances, congressional delegates, tribal

---

[*] C. White, T. Cade, and J. Enderson, *Peregrine Falcons of the World* (Barcelona: Lynx Edicions, 2013).

representatives, and others, Chimney Rock received permanent protection at last. On September 21, 2012, President Barack Obama, using executive authority under the 1906 Antiquities Act, proclaimed, set apart, and reserved Chimney Rock as a national monument. This designation distinguishes the 4,726-acre Chimney Rock Archaeological Area for its natural, cultural, and historical significance. The National Trust for Historic Preservation, which began the campaign to designate the area a national monument, has labeled Chimney Rock as the most important cultural site to be managed by the U.S. Forest Service. Thousands of people have applauded this action, including the Southern Ute Indians, whose reservation surrounds Chimney Rock. Together with all Native American Puebloans, they are especially grateful for the president's decision to guard their sacred, ancestral site in perpetuity.

There are stories in life that need to be remembered and retold, again and again. They point out our responsibilities, as human beings, to things that have no voice—to species and places that matter—and that can't be saved without our help. The remarkable accounts of the rescue of the peregrine falcon and the preservation of Chimney Rock are two such tales. Both are a testament to the human spirit. They show we can—and *do*—make a difference.

But they tell us something more: not to forget our past. Today, there are other important places in need of protection and more species facing critical situations. By working to save them, we all benefit, especially future generations. Yet as these stories also show, sometimes that aim seems impossible. The challenge is, how do we proceed, especially when hope looks dim?

. . . The splendid bird that just flew over my head in my pasture answered that question once and for all: *Never Give Up.*

Chapter One

 THE SCREAM CAME FROM OVERHEAD. The black dart hurtled above the ledge then disappeared in a dive to the earth. I was awake instantly. The air was cold for the third of June. I tried to dress in my sleeping bag, then gave up and jumped up half naked. The sickle-shaped flying image was gone—I couldn't find it with my binoculars because they were fogged and icy from being left out in the cold. The opportunity I had waited for all night was gone.

The falcon had left for its morning hunt. Who knew when it would be back? And I was a mile and a half from my car, camping gear, food, and water, and most of my scientific equipment. Blowing into my hands didn't help assuage the chill, so I jumped up and down, which immediately aroused the suspicions of a rock wren who apparently held title to the ledge I had usurped last night. He scolded fiercely, then paused to watch as I dressed; unlike me, the bird was oblivious of the one-thousand-foot drop-off within ten feet of us.

The panoramic view from the windy promontory was too grand to take in. It was too stark and foreign, especially when compared to the city of Colorado Springs and the life I had just left. The mountain on which I stood rose twelve hundred feet from the surrounding valley floor, and in that vertical distance the eye was taken through several vegetation zones. At the bottom were rolling foothills, pastel gray and green with sagebrush and scrub oak; then, higher, emerald forests of ponderosa pine and Douglas fir; and finally, blue side slopes of Colorado spruce and subalpine fir. I looked, as if from an airplane, at silver threads that represented rivers and at purple dots passing for lakes far below. The scene had everything—miles and miles of it—everything except people. This part of southwestern Colorado was dominated by fourteen-thousand-foot mountains. People were scarce and lived in small towns tucked away in isolated valleys.

But it wasn't people that I wanted just now, I reminded myself, with not just a hint of loneliness; it was something else, rare and unsociable—a spark of creation that preferred the highest cliffs and farthest wilderness, the fastest living creature on earth, a species that had inhabited the world for at least twenty-nine thousand years, though it was questionable if it would survive another thirty.

A startling cry, "Killy, Killy, Killy," came from below me, making me jump, and the blue, tapering wings and brilliant orange tail of a male kestrel cut through the sky almost at my feet. How peculiar, how very peculiar to see things flying below you. I must grow accustomed to viewing birds from this unusually high vantage point and to identifying them from their tops, not their undersides. Following closely behind the kestrel was a red-tailed hawk, with its russet tail fanning. Its dusty white breast and black belly band were obscured from view as it dipped down beneath the ledge and disappeared.

I threw on my down jacket and, my fingers stiff with cold, began assembling the spotting scope atop the five-foot-tall wooden tripod. Several mule deer grazed the serviceberry bushes on the hills below; a badger popped its head out of a hole, sniffed the air, and disappeared again.

My empty stomach growled as I pulled on my pants. Four months: that equated to sixteen weeks, or one hundred and twenty days. That seemed an incredibly long time for someone to live in the wilderness, even for one who enjoyed the adventure of far flung places; I mustn't think about it now.

Suddenly came another sound, a whipping noise like still air sliced by a heaving, sharpened blade. Quickly I strained to focus on an object moving swiftly toward Chimney Rock, the rising sandstone pinnacle that capped the mountain and for which it was named. I heard within seconds a cry, then a second one in response, and through my binoculars saw two peregrine falcons racing at great speed to greet one another. Meeting it in a graceful, swirling motion that seemed but one fluid movement, one falcon flipped upside down to grasp something that the other was carrying. The bird then twisted back to Chimney Rock with its bounty while the other returned to circle above me, wailing in displeasure.

So the gamble had paid off: the peregrine had returned sooner than I expected. Once again I felt the thrill I always did for this creature, *Falco peregrinus anatum*, the American peregrine falcon. Because of its beauty, power, and courage, the peregrine has been a natural symbol of aspiration and freedom for people throughout the ages. Although I was not a falconer, I knew it was this thrill that underscored the sport of falconry, where man became as one with his bird after long weeks of training it to hunt and willingly return to him on command. The peregrine was the favorite hunting bird among falconers because of its great speed and power and the inherent docility that made it the easiest of all hunting hawks to train.

I found it difficult to fathom the antiquity of the sport. This union of man and bird had originated over four thousand years ago with the ancient Chinese; from there, it had spread throughout the world, reaching by A.D. 600, Korea, Japan, the Middle East, and Central Europe. By the year 919, falconry was already the choice sport of princes and magnates, and by the Middle Ages, it became so esteemed that kings and princes kept their hunting falcons with them at all times, taking them everywhere, even to church and their own weddings. A symbiotic relationship seemed to exist between the peregrine falcon and man. Man admired the peregrine, captured it, taught it to trust him. But at the close of the twentieth century, it was now man's responsibility to give the falcon back its freedom and its life. The alternative was extinction.

I sat down on the hard rock to lace up my boots and realized I would not have the luxury of a chair at my disposal for a long, long time. But it was worth it to me to study one of seven last pairs of wild peregrines surviving in the Rocky Mountains, by living with them during their 1975 nesting season. During this time I hoped to acquire some of the most detailed accounts to date of wild falcon behavior. I would study their life at the nesting site, or eyrie, observe their feeding patterns and hunting tactics, where they preferred to hunt and what they ate. I would record their interaction with their young and with other bird species and also their reactions to variations in weather, noise, and aircraft, and to man. From these data I hoped to document their habitat requirements and produce recommendations to aid in their management.

The fact that I was only twenty-one years old, an untested wildlife biologist straight from college, didn't seem of consequence to me, but apparently it made a difference to some people. The day before at the local Forest Service office I had expected a welcome reception when I introduced myself and asked to see Mr. Preston Fitch, an administrator involved with the project. Barry Layne, senior biologist with the Colorado

Division of Wildlife and my supervisor, had explained that the peregrines were nesting on Forest Service land, and I took for granted that federal officials would be enthusiastic in cooperating with us in the study.

But upon hearing my business, the secretary's smile sunk. And, as I sat down in the lobby to wait, several heads glanced over in my direction as she passed by them, murmuring and swinging her long, blonde hair. After several minutes, a slight of build, middle-aged man appeared, his chestnut eyes set in a frown. Smiling, I rose to meet him for I knew this must be Mr. Fitch.

"Barry Layne sent *you?*" he asked.

"Yes."

He shook his head. "Why, you can't be more than a college freshman. You're much too young for this kind of work. I will speak to Mr. Layne later today."

I had faith Barry would stand behind me, but I was still embarrassed because the secretary and several men were within earshot and grinning broadly while they sipped at coffee.

"Have you seen Chimney Rock?" Mr. Fitch continued. I answered him that I had, once, on a training trip earlier in the spring with Barry Layne and Dr. James Enderson.

"Well, in any case, I'll accompany you today. I've business to look into near there, and we can discuss what you may need in supplies—that is, if you stay."

Mr. Fitch walked briskly back to his office, leaving me standing awkwardly. His concern was understandable, but I did not appreciate the amusement of the coffee-sipping foresters. I could overhear them taking bets on how long I'd last, and when I left the office five minutes later with Mr. Fitch, their "Give 'er one week" reverberated through my ears, both as a reproach and a challenge.

Travelling with Mr. Fitch was a lesson in patience. He had insisted I go with him in the same car, which was inefficient, since it meant I had to drive back into town again, an hour away, pick up my own car, then retrace my steps. After a stop at the Job Corps Center, where he collected some camping gear, he misplaced the car keys then spent a half hour looking for them. Conversation between us was restrained; he answered my questions with monosyllables or with a grunt, as if he were trying to clear his throat. After an hour of being together, I had just about proclaimed Mr. Fitch incapable of enthusiasm about anything, but I was mistaken, for suddenly he smiled to himself as he pulled off the road to an old farmhouse.

"Why are we stopping here?"

"This will only take a minute." Without another word, he climbed out of the truck as two men approached. After a brief welcome, the three began discussing coal mining; apparently a small mining operation was located somewhere behind the house, but what it had to do with the U.S. Forest Service was mystifying. Mr. Fitch soon returned and without any explanation drove off. Curious, I asked him about the mining, and if it was on federal property. Mr. Fitch shook his head.

"Why is the government involved with it then?"

He perked up noticeably. "Because, young lady, underneath this land all around you lies something very important—coal. The entire San Juan Basin will one day be leased for coal development. Millions and millions of tons of coal are just lying underground waiting to be tapped, waiting to make this country come alive. . . ."

He paused and changed the subject. "Now before I forget, don't lose this," he remarked, reaching into his shirt pocket and producing a key. "This is for you. It's federal property, and I've recorded it in your name. It's for the gate to Chimney

Rock. Only a few people have one; the road is closed to public access."

"Why would anyone try to drive up that terrible road? When I came here in the spring, we almost didn't make it to the top, it's so narrow and steep and badly rutted. No one in his right mind—"

"The Forest Service built that road," he said with pride, "and it has already cost us over a half million dollars. Unfortunately, we were forced to discontinue our efforts last year when—when the falcons were found on Chimney Rock."

Fitch pressed down the accelerator and, upon reaching the mountain and passing through the gate, charged up the rough road like a soldier maneuvering a tank. Mud splattered on the doors and windows, and the windshield wipers only smeared the mess. For five miles we contorted side to side, at last reaching the top, where the road leveled and dead ended at a turn around. Hopping out of the truck, Mr. Fitch remarked that he had no time to walk the mile to the observation overlook where I would be working. Quickly he unloaded the water jug, portable stove, and Styrofoam cooler, which he said were on loan for my use.

"Where do you want these?" he asked.

"On the ground's fine."

"Two hundred and fifty."

"Two hundred and fifty?"

"Ruins. There are two hundred and fifty ruins here. Chimney Rock is a designated archeological district. It shelters Anasazi Indian ruins that date from the 900–1100 era."

I had been aware that Chimney Rock was one of the northernmost-known residences of the ancient Anasazi Indians. They had lived in this harsh wind-swept land for centuries. By their ingenuity and persistence, they had achieved an astounding level of culture by A. D. 1000, surpassing all other prehistoric American Indian tribes north of Mexico. At Mesa Verde, Colorado, only a couple hours' drive from here, were hundreds of cliff dwellings that hung to cliffs like swallow nests, testifying to the Anasazi's phenomenal engineering skills. The Chimney Rock site was dated earlier, was more primitive. I was intrigued.

"Remember to stay back from the edge at the top," Mr. Fitch said as he motioned for me to get in the truck. "This creates a great deal of inconvenience. I wasn't planning on putting up safety rails until later this summer. But that was before. Before I knew about you."

Chapter Two

 BY THE END of that first day, I forgot all about Mr. Fitch. By the end of the second, I found I had to put aside many of the suppositions I had about life as a wildlife biologist. What you never learn in college biology class or see on television is that for every hour a wildlife scientist has actually observed his subject doing anything at all exciting, he has probably spent ten times that amount of time sitting and waiting. And waiting.

The primary qualification for a field biologist is patience. After five hours of work on my first afternoon in the field, all I had observed was:

That, in my note-taking shorthand, meant:

bird left perch ( )

and disappeared ( ).

The art of taking field notes was something at which I would soon become extremely proficient, but at the start I had not memorized all the symbols that Dr. James Enderson and

I had devised. So, at first the code did not streamline the task of recording observations, as it was meant to do. Instead, I had to write down each activity twice—once in longhand, then once again in symbols, after referring to my notes to figure out what the symbols meant.

It was a good system in theory. Instead of using the standard yellow, pocket-sized notebook carried by all biologists, I chose to fill each day one eight-by-eleven-inch sheet of paper, dividing this up into a grid to be covered with shorthand. On the left hand side of the paper, going down the page, were the hours of my typical observer day—0500–2100 hours. Across the page, each hour was divided up into five-minute intervals, leaving 204 little squares to be filled in with symbols. At the top of each page was a space for recording the hourly ambient temperature, wind, and, if applicable, precipitation.

												MIN.
HRS.	5	10	15	20	25	30	35	40	45	50	55	60
0500												
0600												
0700												
0800												
0900												
1000												
1100												
1200												
1300												
1400												
1500												
1600												
1700												
1800												
1900												
2000												
2100												

The fourteen symbols I used denoted the major functions of a peregrine falcon's life at home:

↰ —left perch

⌁ —flying

@ —circling high

w◯e —cardinal direction bird flew from cliff
N
S

↓ —diving

人 —preening

Ⱳ —wailing

⅗ —defensive diving at intruders

Ƙ —disappeared from view

✝ —returned to cliff

✝ —returned to cliff with prey in talons

⌁ —food exchange (male giving female food)

$\frac{1}{4}$ —perching (number denotes perch location on cliff)

☉ —eating

◁— —returned to eyrie

The symbols were also color coded: blue for the male falcon, or tiercel, and red for the female, or falcon. At first I was forced to add a third color—brown—for when I couldn't tell the difference. Veteran falconers can easily differentiate between male and female birds from more than a half mile away, but I was not a veteran yet. The difference is not in coloration or general appearance. In peregrine falcons, both sexes have the same long, pointed wings, sleek and highly maneuverable; the same slate gray-blue backs and lightly streaked white breasts; the look of pride in their sharp brown eyes; and jet black facial markings suggesting a helmet crowning their bullet shaped heads.

What differentiates the two is their size. Peregrines are unlike many species of mammals and birds in which the male is the larger, more visible sex. Falcons, and most birds of prey, are characterized by reversed-size dimorphism, in which the female of the species is the larger of the two. Female peregrines in fact are a full third larger and 50 percent heavier than their male counterparts and can take larger prey, which endears them to old-time falconers, who prefer them over males for hunting, and out of respect call only the female bird falcon.

The male, although an equally swift and brilliant flier, is relegated to the more unglamorous term tiercel, meaning "third."

After sitting down for most of the day, I got up to stretch and mentally made note of the first unspoken law of wildlife science: when the subject of the scientist's attention does nothing for hours, the other species of the area, those he is not recording, perform one antic after another. At least this was true from my vantage point on the exposed ledge, where more than fifty white-throated swifts were propelling themselves close by my head like miniature jet fighters in active combat.

The whistle and whir of their sturdy little wings grazing past my body was more than a little unnerving, though they never actually struck me in their mad quest for insects, which also were out en masse. Hundreds of gnats and mosquitoes buzzed around my body as soon as the wind calmed and the sun began baking the cliff. And this was particularly annoying, for the one thing I had neglected to bring with me to Chimney Rock was insect repellent.

Other wildlife was more quiet, but equally apparent. A yellow-bellied marmot was whistling alarm from a hole, half hidden by a blooming cliff-fendler bush; several pairs of colorful mountain bluebirds darted across the backdrop of the tall Douglas firs on the north slope; herds of elk and deer grazed in the secluded valleys hundreds of feet below.

But the peregrines were out of my sight. My pacing up and down on the ledge failed to elicit any response from the falcons, though I knew they could see me clearly. I was only a quarter mile from their eyrie on Chimney Rock, and peregrine falcon vision is superb, even legendary. With a visual acuity two to eight times that of the average man, peregrines can spot small prey from over two miles away. From their quiet I deduced two things: one, that the tiercel was probably away hunting, and two, the falcon was brooding newly hatched young and did not dare to leave them.

It was still early June, but the nesting cycle for peregrine falcons had begun weeks earlier, when the birds returned to the cliffs in late March for their yearly courtship proceedings. Usually by mid-April, egg-laying starts in earnest, extending over a period of about twenty days, when a clutch of three or four eggs is laid. Eggs hatch in thirty-three days, but in the meantime must be continually incubated. Males contribute substantially to the process. They incubate the eggs for a third of the entire time, which means that eggs are left unattended only for very short periods—generally less than three minutes—while the birds change shifts. For the rest of the day, males hunt food for their hungry mates.

After the eggs hatch—the stage I suspected the birds were at now—the male spends considerably less time at the eyrie, for his attention is now directed toward searching for food for the growing brood. The female at this time is often left alone to guard the nest of helpless chicks covered with delicate white down, their half-closed eyes unseeing until they are four days old. For at least sixteen days the nestlings will mostly sleep, protected from predators, rain and sun by the unceasing vigilance of their mother. This predictable cycle has been going on for generations of peregrines. Now it is possibly in its final stage.

Peregrines, though never prolific, were not an uncommon sight before 1940 for the keen birdwatcher scouting mountainous cliffs and river gorges. But by the mid-1970's, the American peregrine falcon, whose original range stretched from the Atlantic to the Pacific in every state of the Union, almost disappeared. Where once hundreds of wild peregrines nested east of the Mississippi River, by 1975 none remained. In the western U.S. a few residual pair were left in Oregon, 20 or so in California, and in the Rockies, where there had been over 180 nesting pairs, only a few stragglers were left. The same tragic story was true for peregrines around the world. By 1963, their population in Western Europe and Great Britain had been cut in half; in Sweden by 1965, only 350 of the thousand pairs remained, by the mid 1970s, only four.

Yet it was not until the late 1940's that scientists around the world began suspecting things were going awry for the peregrine. By 1960, when the spectre of extinction was looming over the species, biologists were racing in desperation to uncover the mysterious reason for the plunging decline in productivity, to explain why eggs were not hatching, why they were breaking, and why adult peregrines were abandoning nest sites used for generations but were not showing up anywhere else.

The breakthrough came almost simultaneously in Britain and in the United States. Derek Radcliffe, noted British researcher, after observing an ugly sight that deeply bothered him—a wild mother falcon eating her own egg—began to closely examine and compare peregrine eggshells collected in the 1960's with those preserved in collections from earlier dates. He came to the startling conclusion that peregrine eggshells after 1946 were 25 percent thinner than they normally had been.

Radcliffe relayed his discovery to Dr. Joseph Hickey of the University of Wisconsin, who in turn began analyzing thousands of peregrine eggshells in America. Hickey came to the same conclusion. Both men recognized that this single fact was highly significant in causing the peregrine's decline. Because peregrines build no nest but instead lay their eggs on rocky bare ledges, called scrapes, their eggs are under considerable stress during incubation. With significantly thinned shells the eggs are not able to sustain their parents' weight and movement, and break before they hatch.

But what was the reason for the thinning? Why was it occurring? Scientists working around the world discovered that the culprits were widely used but appalling substances, chlorinated hydrocarbons, primarily the pesticide DDT.

DDT usage became widespread after 1940. In a mere ten years time, in a quiet but lethal fashion, the seemingly innocuous, but actually very toxic chemical worked its way up the food chain, leaving in its wake a stream of death. Small birds, ingesting insects that fed on vegetation laced with DDT poison, concentrated it in their bodies; birds at the top of the food chain, such as the peregrine, feeding on these smaller birds, inadvertently concentrated larger and larger doses of the pesticide in their systems.

At this level of toxicity, DDE, which is the first chemical produced in the breakdown of DDT, wreaked havoc on the peregrine's reproductive system. It lowered the blood level of estrogen, the female hormone, thus inhibiting the production of calcium in their bodies. When DDE reached twenty parts per million in the peregrine's blood, the falcon's eggs began decreasing in thickness by 15 to 20 percent. The eggs began to break.

Other birds, however, were less sensitive to the pesticide and masked the agent's toxicity. Ducks and gulls, for example, didn't experience reproductive failure until DDE levels were considerably higher—one hundred parts per million. But in the sensitive peregrines, when DDE levels went above twenty ppm, gruesome results occurred. The birds' nervous systems began to be destroyed. Their parental behavior went haywire. The once stable falcon began abandoning her nest full of eggs or merely refused to incubate them, so the eggs never hatched. Even worse were shocking behavioral changes such as the dedicated parent eating her own eggs.

In June 1970, the American peregrine falcon was declared an endangered species. Because of conclusive evidence that DDT was responsible for the destruction of a species, the pesticide was banned in 1972 in the United States. The interdict was hailed as a good start. But the question still lingered: had it come too late?

Suddenly I heard the recognizable alarm call I had been waiting for, jangling me to attention. Before me a peregrine falcon emerged from the cliff with a fierce beauty; with utmost ease and perfect control, it spun in a dizzying dive to the earth. Talons outstretched, it lightly grazed the object of its attention—a trespassing prairie falcon who had slipped across the peregrine's invisible territorial line. The peregrine, wings tightly pressed along its body, then bulleted to tremendous heights and with an even wilder drive, sailed again at the prairie falcon. Just before contact, however, it braked, recovering with perfect backward rolls while looping upwards to the sky. Its flight was a gust of pure energy: one minute tempered, held in position, the next second a bolt of lightning striking this way and that—high, low, making mad twirls in the air— fast, slow, a crescendo of motion, and then, it was all over. The prairie falcon had retreated, and the peregrine was sitting proudly atop the cliff, surveying its world.

I slumped over the spotting scope, awestruck from the exhibition. This bird was not a ghost; it was real, and I knew that this was the place I wanted to be more than any other. Once again I felt the truth of Dr. Enderson's words: The land and cliffs and sky can never again mean quite the same thing for one who has witnessed a peregrine in flight.

Chapter Three

ONE HAS TO BECOME like a falcon, to think like him in a way, for the bird to accept one's presence, and this I tried to do from the start by becoming a predictable entity—walking to the observation post at the same time, in the same way every day, dressed always in familiar clothes, my slow, measured movements following an anticipated pattern. With no one to see or talk to, after only three days I had come to know the peregrines on fairly intimate terms. I recognized immediately that the official lord of Chimney Rock was the male falcon. He was a valiant, intelligent-looking creature, of medium size, 15 inches in length, 1.5 to 2.5 pounds, similar to a crow. He confirmed his courage on my second day out when I observed him taking off from the cliff, crying a violent "Kak-Kak-Kak" that disrupted the stillness of the mountain and circling high into the air, his wingtips moving sensitively with finger-like motions. Upon reaching an elevation twice the height of Chimney Rock, he stooped like a released arrow upon a bird twice his size, a golden eagle.

Eagles are the most despised adversaries of peregrines. They are destroyers of peregrine nests, for they occasionally feed on falcon young. I realized that this male falcon was fiercely attempting to drive this enemy from his territory. The peregrine circled up, then dove a second time on the eagle, but the large bird merely rolled over on its back, thrusting out its own talons in retaliation. Undaunted, the tiercel grasped the eagle's talons, sending both birds downward in a spiraling fighting grip. The eagle was the first to break away and defiantly continued his encroachment on the eyrie.

He didn't get far. From the direction of the cliff there came another cry, deeper, more urgent. In frantic flight, the female peregrine shot from the eyrie to defend her nest. Reaching her mate, she became a single force with him against the eagle. Like two sickles in a duet of motion, they cut across each other's path. Defending himself against these two was suddenly more difficult than the eagle had expected; he tried rolling over on one side to avoid being hit by one, but was immediately assailed amidships on his unprotected flank by the other. After several minutes, realizing his defeat, the eagle suddenly pulled his wings close aside his body and retreated in a downward glide to the east, with the dauntless tiercel continuing the pursuit for an additional mile.

Satisfied, the female falcon glissaded back to Chimney Rock, but before returning to the eyrie and her nestlings, she perched on the crest of the cliff. Viewing her closely through a spotting scope, I noted that her glossy appearance was the more dramatic of the two peregrines. The falcon's coal black hood covered almost her entire head and was not merely the typical facial moustache, and her size and regal bearing were exceptional even for a female peregrine. These traits more closely resembled the peregrine falcons that had lived on the eastern coast of North America—a race of birds now completely wiped out.

There is a special quality about some peregrines—a look in the eye, a kind of aristocratic stance, a fine-detailing of plumage—that according to falconers, makes them stand out as the champions of the bird world. Only an expert, one who has observed and worked with peregrines for many years, can detect these things, for the traits are not written down; but falconers say the fact is indisputable. Both Dr. Enderson and Barry Layne agreed that this falcon of Chimney Rock was of that winning breed. Watching her, I remembered a story Dr. Enderson had told me about this very female. He and another peregrine advocate, Mike Brewer, had observed her early in the spring during the time of pre-nesting courtship activities. It is well known that peregrine falcons mate for life, but as they witnessed, that fact doesn't always discourage an occasional unmated bird from vying for a possible mate.

In early April, they had observed a third peregrine falcon, another female, mainlining into the territory of the Chimney Rock falcons in brazen defiance of the two that already had created their "pair bond." Perturbed, the matron of Chimney Rock blasted from the cliff to attack the intruder, skimming by her with jutting, threatening talons. A marvelous flier herself, the new female was undaunted. She avoided the attacks by twisting skillfully and bypassed her opponent to race closer to the cliff, sweeping past and displaying for the male.

Wailing in her distress, the resident bird stepped up her defense, but she was unprepared when the invading bird suddenly tacked and viciously began assailing her. The motive was easily apparent: this new bird was attempting to win the tiercel and Chimney Rock for herself.

Proving her courage, the tiring, defending falcon refused to give in. The two female peregrines plummeted headlong at each other, one after the other rising 500 feet or more to prepare for another stoop. Cutting beneath each other, both would then try for fighting positions that enabled them to curve up and attack from below. As minutes passed, the attacks became fiercer, and it became evident that, though a truly brilliant flier, the Chimney Rock falcon was losing.

Suddenly the unexpected happened. Soundlessly, the tiercel took off. With lightning speed he gashed the sky to dive upon the intruder, his quick, agile movements far too fast for her to defend against. Unrelenting, the tiercel masterfully battled her from all sides until he had succeeded in driving the bird completely from the vicinity. Only then did he return to the cliff and perch peaceably, as if nothing had happened. His beautiful, exhausted mate seemed overjoyed in her relief. With renewed vigor, she dived and soared, tore around and around the Rock, executing one loop after another, in a flight that spelled her glorious victory.

This exhibition proved again the tenacity of the falcon pair bond. Peregrines, like these of Chimney Rock, establish lively histories together for periods of seven to ten years, sometimes more. Usually the two will separate for a short while in the winter, though some have been observed staying together throughout the year, never roosting or venturing far from each other. It is only when a partner dies that the survivor may take a new mate. For all their monogamy, however, matrimonial bliss does not always come easily. Early in their courtship, peregrines must make social adjustments. Female peregrines can often be domineering creatures who insist upon having their way in matters such as the right time for copulation, where the eyrie should be placed on the cliff, or when the tiercel should hunt for more food. Already I had witnessed the Chimney Rock falcon using her feminine wiles to tell her mate she was hungry: she would fly up behind him, strike him forcibly from his perch, and then he was usually on his way.

In most things the falcons seemed to work together, but they were especially dependent on each other to raise their family. Every day the tiercel traveled miles from Chimney Rock in all directions searching for food; apparently all the land that surrounded the cliff he considered his domain. That included the slow, winding San Juan River that laced like a silver thread to the southwest, the deep-green forested canyons in the southeastern distance, and the observation ridge with all the Anasazi Indian ruins that Mr. Fitch had pointed out with such pride.

There was something inherently majestic and mysterious about these birds, and soon I began to appreciate the fascination they held for the generations of falconers who had lived with them, cared for them, made them the passion of their lives. In the thirteenth century, Emperor Frederick II brought some falcons and their trainers back with him after his travels to Asia and pronounced falconry the noblest of all arts. For the next four-hundred years, the peregrine was the nobleman's hawk, esteemed and protected by severe penalties. Falcon motifs began showing up on tapestries, jewelry, and fine carvings.

A well-trained falcon had an inexplicable bond with its master, waiting high in the air for him to flush prey and then, totally free, stooping to strike it for him, at last returning, by his own volition, to his trainer's fist. Just as the falcon was mysteriously tied to its handler, a true falconer was always devoted to his birds. Some became so much so, in fact, that during the Middle Ages, the Roman Catholic church actually forbade its priests to pursue the sport of falconry. It was deemed too tempting and too easily could lure a holy man away from his service to God. Fortunately, the edict didn't last long, and priests were once again given the freedom to fly their falcons.

With the invention of gunpowder, however, everything changed. Attitudes shifted entirely; falcons were now regarded as competitors for game birds sought by gun-wielding hunters. All the protection for falcons dissolved; by the end of the seventeenth century, birds of prey became like wanted criminals, and it is only until this day that opinions are beginning to shift once again in their favor.

With all this history behind them, I was finding it extremely difficult to call the peregrines of Chimney Rock simply "A" and "B," as I had been instructed to do—"scientific objectivity" and all that. They didn't at all behave like an "A" or a "B." "A," still tired and harassed from chasing the eagle, was now being teased by a pair of ravens that lived 150 feet below the falcons. The ravens knew their limits—they were not allowed any closer than 100 feet from the peregrine eyrie—but every once in a while, just for fun, they enjoyed taunting their overlords. Just now it was a variation on the theme of leapfrog: one raven flew a fraction of a foot above the "safe" zone. The second, with a careful eye above him, flew just a bit higher. The falcon didn't budge. The first raven, growing in his boldness, flapped higher still, jesting the peregrine with a "croak."

The croak did it. Instantly, the peregrine dived off, scattering the frightened ravens who rushed to hide behind the cliff.

No, "A" and "B" would not do. With a flash of insight, I knew the tiercel had to be named after the monarch who had loved falconry above everything: King Arthur. Of course, then it followed that his mate should be Guinevere. Jenny. I would call her Jenny.

I sat back relaxed, pleased with my idea. The names were perfect. But never would I tell Barry Layne; he already thought that I was too much of a romantic. Which I was. That was inexcusable in a scientist, especially when that scientist was a woman. But it never seemed to bother the falcons, and they kept my secret, until the day Barry commented, "I don't know how you can be so damned impartial about these birds. You'd think anyone who lived with them as long as you would at least give them some names. So I guess I'll have to name them for you—Stanley and Irene."

Chapter Four

THE DAY EVERYTHING TURNED upside down at Chimney Rock began with a simple favor from Mr. Fitch. He was only being kind. But the repercussions would eventually shatter all my neat and well-intentioned scientific preconceptions of how things should act and react, of what was right and what wasn't. The fit of things was never quite comfortable again, like a shoe that is either too large or too tight. And even the adjustments of the cobbler never again allow you to walk quite unconscious of your feet.

I had lived a week alone. And I was completely unprepared for the shock of hearing another voice coming from behind me on the mountain. Whirling around I faced a short, red-faced, muscular man swinging a hammer in his fist.

"For God's sake, lady, don't look at me like that! All I said was hello. You should be ashamed of yourself for spying on Tweety Bird, you know. If I was Tweety and you was watching me, I'd move to another district."

"Who . . . who are you?"

"Rude. You're very rude. Most biologists are, I've noticed. Anyhow, I've as much right as you to be here. I've been given orders from Mr. Fitch to build you a lookout—for your protection, of course."

"You're with the Forest Service?"

"And you're not very smart either. Who else would be up here? You and your biology friends have got this place so barred up to pacify poor little Tweety that you need special permission from the president of the United States to set foot in the shrine."

"What do you mean, protection?"

"Lady, in July that there sun will bake that cliff you're sitting on to a burned biscuit."

I pulled the big yellow hat I wore farther down on my head. Already I was sunburned, and I once again regretted my blonde hair and fair skin. The man sauntered over to the tumbled-down fire tower that was positioned just behind the ledge on which I was sitting and where I had spent my first night. All that remained of the obsolete structure was a brick rectangular base that stood about ten feet high. He kicked the foundation like he was testing worn tires.

"This here thing is your new home. You'll be Mrs. Marlin Perkins óf Animal Kingdom."

"Really, I appreciate your offer, but you don't have
to go to all this trouble."

"I do so, whether I like it or not, because Fitch said so. Now you'll be able to invade poor Tweety Bird's privacy even better. Personally, I think it's pretty disgusting, you nosing around these two animals, never allowing them a moment to themselves. How would you like that? But speaking of trouble, the last time I saw the other fellas they were having a hell of a time with your trailer."

"My what?"

"Trailer. Didn't you know? Fitch said you've got to have a trailer—'No young missy is going to sleep outside on the bare ground for four months,' or something like that. Of course, we all disagreed: any fool doing what you're doing deserves the ground. But don't say you don't need a trailer, 'cause you got it. Cheer up; it's the worst we got. It's dented, there's no toity, no water, and the stove don't work. Look at it this way, it should protect you during the lightning storms, if you can get to it fast enough. Up here, that's doubtful."

Confused, I sat back and covered my notes with my pack so they would not blow away. In the distance, I heard a terrible grinding noise, something like metal against metal, that was getting closer.

"It's coming. Better get back to the truck. It's nothing but a crime to drag that poor old thing up this road."

I cringed and, lagging several feet behind, followed the man down the trail. Back at his truck, he began unloading pieces of two by fours.

"May I help you carry something?" I asked.

"You?" He made a comment about my scrawniness. Undaunted, I grabbed up the hammers and a sack of nails and followed him back up the trail. After a half mile, he stopped, groaning, and dropped the boards.

"I swear they grow two by fours heavier every year. Well, have a seat; don't just stand there staring—you make me nervous." Wiping his brow with the back of his hand, he grabbed two cigarettes from his hip pocket and offered me one. I shook my head.

"So you're a health nut too. Tell me something, bird lady. Just what's so special about this Tweety anyhow? He don't look much different than a common old crow if you ask me."

The question caught me off guard. Right away, I couldn't answer it, because in the whole scheme of things the peregrine actually wasn't really any more important than a crow or any other living creature. Aesthetically, of course, it was considerably more glamorous; it was beautiful to look at, graceful and swift—in a fast dive it could exceed speeds of two hundred miles an hour. Also, it had thousands of years of history interwoven with man. But in terms of extinction, all species held equal weight. Once a species was gone, it was gone for good— a peregrine, a whooping crane, a condor.

I wanted to say something about the horror of the projected species loss we would see in our lifetime. The disappearance of the dinosaurs or other creatures in evolutionary time was nothing like what would happen by the end of our century. Now the rate of extinction was four hundred times greater than at anytime in the past. By the year 2000, scientists anticipated that five hundred thousand to one million species would disappear from the earth all because of one force—human beings. The peregrine, the crow—we were responsible for them all because we were the ones in control. Each distinct species saved was a triumph; each lost was a tremendous loss for all future generations of man.

My pause made the man comment that he knew I couldn't answer his simple question.

"You'd never be any good at a game show. Okay, bird lady, numero two. You're a nice looking girl; you don't seem as nasty as most biologists. So why do you want to do this? You have a thing against people, or what?"

I faced him with surprise. What was he talking about? It was a privilege to have this job.

"A privilege? Well bully for you. You're one tough broad." Throwing his cigarette down, he heaved up the boards on his shoulder and strode on, not looking back. When at last he reached the fire tower, he scattered the load.

"One thing that bugs the hell out of me is a person trying to act cute. You know damned well what I'm talking about."

"I have no idea what you're talking about."

"You're asking me to believe they sent you out here without telling you anything?" He paused to scrutinize my face. "This road here—did you think they built it just so you could watch Tweety?"

"Why of course not."

"Well, they sure as hell didn't. This community and the Forest Service have spent close to a fortune carving it into this mountain. We built it because we plan to turn Chimney Rock into one of the best tourist attractions in the state. In the whole Southwest."

Looking about me, I found myself asking the same question I had asked when I had noticed Mr. Fitch's interest in the small coal mine: Why here? What was here? Remembering Mr. Fitch's pride in the Indian relics, I wondered if the tourist development had anything to do with the Anasazi ruins.

"The plans call for Chimney Rock to be developed like Mesa Verde," he said, livening up. "Over a million tourists a year visit that place, and they spend money—that mean anything to you? If Chimney Rock gets a fraction of that, the place would be a hell of an improvement."

With a national park like Mesa Verde so close by, I asked why we needed a second development. Unquestionably, Mesa Verde was far more spectacular than Chimney Rock.

Instantly I realized I'd intimated the wrong thing.

"Like hell it's better. Our development's going to be hundreds of acres, with trailer parks, visitor centers, refreshment stands, and even a tramway. Mesa Verde doesn't have that. It'll run all the way from down there to up here where we're standing. So your little Tweety Bird better not spoil everything. If he does, we might do something about it."

Flexing his arm, he held the hammer almost under my nose.

"Tell me this, how come all the years we've been planning this thing, Tweety never bothered nesting on Chimney Rock? How come only now, when the road's almost in and everybody's ready to get underway, Tweety decides he wants to make his homey here? And then some endangered species hogwash steps in and grinds the whole development to a stop, 'cause Tweety might get his feelings hurt."

He slowly lowered the tool and spit on the ground. "Poor damn Tweety."

I didn't follow the man as he headed down the trail but waited with a blend of dread and impatience for him and his friends to return and get the building of the lookout over. Observing the peregrine's reactions to the increased activity, I noted that Jenny vented her anger over the man's intrusion by striking out at the poor ravens, who this time had done nothing to warrant such behavior and who huddled together in silent terror next to their nest.

In less than a half-hour, I was aware of heavy footsteps and huffing and puffing. Three over-exerted men, one, the previous visitor, were dragging canvas sheets and a pile of boards behind them.

"Towing that trailer's like dragging an elephant up this road. Stuck twice as we rounded the final turn. Should have dumped it."

Jumping up, I apologized for the inconvenience I'd caused, but they appeared not to hear me.

"How are you going to live up here with no running water or refrigerator?" one of the men asked. I explained that I kept my food, my perishable food, in a cooler Mr. Fitch loaned me and that I had my water in a five-gallon jug.

"Five gallons don't go too far. What you going to do after that?"

"Hey, Bill, I've got the perfect solution. She could go to the Lost Canyon Cafe. That's only ten miles from here. It would be better than driving all the way back to town. Unless, of course, she, being an ecology person, prefers doing it the natural way. Then she could hike down two thousand feet to the river and carry it on her back." All three men went into paroxysms at this.

"The Lost Canyon Cafe will be fine, thanks," I replied quietly.

For the next hour the men kept to themselves, constructing a wooden platform to balance on the ten-foot-high fire tower's old foundation. Each time a board dropped, the peregrines reacted violently by screaming out "Kak-Kak-Kak," their loud, repetitious vocalization for anything that provoked extreme anxiety. Nesting peregrines will not tolerate lengthy or excessive human encroachment near the nesting site. Often, too much disturbance before the eggs are laid will result in abandonment of the nest.

Just this once, I was not overly concerned about the disturbance, for the peregrines were well entrenched in their nesting cycle. Yet I could see that it would not be a good thing if it went on too long. When the workmen announced they were finished, I was relieved.

Climbing down the ladder, all three stopped to observe their work with satisfaction on their faces. I was pleased to see that they had fashioned the canvas tarp into a roof for the top of the platform, which would shield me from the glaring sun.

"We'll leave this ladder with you, unless you think you can fly up there."

I looked up the ten feet and laughed. "No; no I can't."

"Well maybe you're human after all. We've met some biologist types who think they're God, telling us what to do. I'd like to see them jump off this cliff and try to fly. They'd learn pretty fast what they can't do."

"Um, thank you. It looks great. A real improvement."

"Thank Fitch, not us," said the tall, sinewy man who had wrangled with the trailer. "We're just paid to follow his orders. By the way, he said he wants to see you in town. Pronto."

Oh what now. Checking my spotting scope, I faced the Rock. The men gathered their tools and prepared to leave. I turned to say good-by, but two had already begun down the trail; only the one I'd talked to earlier hung back, eyeing Chimney Rock. Bending over to grip his faded red cap, he tossed it once into the air, caught it, and fondled it meditatively. Finally he shook his head and laughed out loud.

"Look, bird lady, if you take everything personally that's said around here, you'll never last. I'll tell you one thing, now that no one but Tweety can hear me, on my part, I like you. You've got to have some sort of guts or you wouldn't be here. But you're going to need a lot, lady. A lot of guts."

He slapped the cap on his round head. "I hope you have them."

Chapter Five

I COULD NOT, absolutely could not go to town to see Mr. Fitch and report that I had not figured out how to open the trailer door. Whether the workmen had done it intentionally, as a little joke, or it was just someone's oversight, they had left the trailer door sporting a shiny new, tightly locked padlock— with no key.

It was, however, the only new thing on the entire trailer. The globular structure was even more pathetic than the workman had described; it wasn't just lightly dented, it was bent. I searched for a key where they had been but found discarded nails and nothing else. Next I checked the windows for a way in; they were bolted and covered with plastic, floral curtains.

It was ridiculous! I paced in front of the thing, every so often stopping at the door to shake or kick it, somehow believing that the padlock must magically spring open, but it stubbornly held. Always in the back of my mind I could hear the workmen laughing: "Typical biologist; typical dumb biologist."

Pausing at the trailer's uneven front steps, I decided to think out the problem. After all, what good was a college education, goals of graduate school and research, if one couldn't even figure out how to unlock a simple door? One thing I refused to do was limp into the Forest Service confessing that I had never used the trailer, because I couldn't get in it, and especially now, considering how unpopular the workmen intimated I was.

But of course they were exaggerating. The next time I called Barry Layne I would ask him about the proposed development, which, until now, no one had even breathed a word about. Surely someone should have told me something; surely Barry wouldn't have let me come here alone as some sort of sacrificial lamb.

Yet reflecting on his last words before I left—"I have confidence you'll be able to handle whatever outside problems may or may not arise"—made me suddenly feel not quite so assured.

But one thing really rankled me. Considering that all the workmen were well aware that peregrines were nesting at Chimney Rock, I wondered how many others knew it? Every raptor biologist I knew was almost paranoid about releasing data of peregrine eyrie locations because of the very real fear of tipping off dishonest falconers who might conceivably steal the young from the last few productive sites. There was a black market for smuggled falcons, and buying and selling prized peregrines was a lucrative business. The whole mess was further complicated by what the federal authorities referred to as the "Arab Connection." Many Arabs loved hunting with falcons. It was, as one biologist had said, their "baseball and football." Owning a peregrine was a sign of one's success and prestige, and because many Arabs had easy cash to spare, prices for a smuggled peregrine began at around $10,000 per bird.

The penalty for such a crime was hardly worth mentioning. In fact, it was so minuscule that it seemed to compel, rather than discourage, unethical dealings. Recently a Chicago businessman had illegally purchased two peregrines from an undercover agent for shipment to a sheik he wished to impress. He was arrested, slapped with a misdemeanor charge and a paltry fine of $500, and let go.

Wildlife officers around the world complain that there is not enough staff or money or outcry to curb illegal trafficking and poaching of threatened and endangered species. Animals continue to grow more scarce as programs designed to protect them collapse.

I was aware that the famous peregrine eyrie at Morro Rock, California, had been robbed in 1972 and again the following year. When a new set of climbers disturbed the adult peregrines, the nest was abandoned. The birds, however, returned in 1974, and the state of California hired round-the-clock wardens to protect the nest, using sophisticated detection equipment that had been designed for Vietnam. Where a real danger existed that breeding adults or their young might be captured or destroyed, the hiring of eyrie wardens was proving successful.

I began to be suspicious about whether Barry Layne had placed me here for this very reason. Certainly not. Yet the startling thought made me jump when a red-shafted flicker burst out in song from the nearby pines, its cry sounding just like the hysterical laughter of someone enjoying a great joke at another's expense. Sighing, I got up and devoted my attention again to the blasted lock.

For the first time I noticed the padlock held a striking resemblance to the one fastening the gate of Chimney Rock road. I grasped it, turning it over in my hand to read the engraving upside down. "Property of the US Govt. For official use only."

No, of course it wouldn't work. Following my intuition

anyway, I reached into my pocket for the key Mr. Fitch had given me for the gate. With amazement I watched as it fit precisely into the padlock; turning it ever so slightly snapped the hinge open. Well, so much for the government's idea of security. I wondered what else the key opened.

The door, swollen like a bulging lid of a spoiled can, required all my force to shove free. Once in, however, I immediately questioned why I had ever wanted to get inside in the first place. The smell wafting from the tomb was like putrid, old socks, and the heat radiating from the too-hot-to-touch aluminum walls made stepping into the interior like walking into a preheating oven. To allow ventilation, I pulled back sticky curtains and unlatched the few windows.

In the light, the trailer's interior features became pronounced, and I went over each one. There was a filthy stove that didn't work; a sink, but no running water to fill it; a chipped, round table with two chairs, all covered with crumbs left over from heaven only knows how long ago; a wooden dresser that refused to open; and, in the far back, a small bunkbed covered with transparent plastic sheets which were nearly molten in the heat.

Trying to look on the bright side, I decided it would be an adequate place to store water and food, books and equipment, keeping them from the nosey field mice and packrats. But it would be safer to sleep outside on the ground. The trailer door slammed shut in the wind, and I pushed it open, thankful for the burst of fresh, clean air. Well, I thought, I might as well get it over with—go to town to see Mr. Fitch and hear whatever it was he wanted to tell me, at the same time refilling with much needed water.

Overhead, Arthur screamed out a hollow warning as I started to my car.

Chapter Six

NONE OF THE SECRETARIES was smiling as I stood in the lobby, and I decided that perhaps they, like me, had a headache, aggravated by the close and dusty afternoon. The seven-foot statue of Smokey the Bear towering in the anteroom also appeared to be glowering about something. Presently I felt like glowering back, after the news that for all my special effort, Mr. Fitch was unable to see me due to an unexpected meeting that had come up. He had, however, left a note with his secretary, which rather cryptically informed me that, one, Barry Layne had called and would be travelling down sometime in the next weeks to check up on things, and two, I could look forward to having a partner soon to aid me in my work.

There was nothing more.

Quizzically, I asked the secretary if Mr. Fitch had said anything more about this "partner," but the unsmiling woman shook her head no. She looked Scandinavian, was blonde and well groomed, with a finely sculptured face and features. Looking up and down at my clothes, she meticulously brushed out her long, pleated skirt. The simple gesture made me feel unattractive and unkempt, with my braided hair unwashed for a week, my clothes wrinkled and dusty.

"Is there someplace I could fill up my water jug?"

She pointed to the restroom.

Lugging the awkward container with me, I fumbled to the bathroom, overhearing starlings and English sparrows calling from outside its open window. The contrast to Chimney Rock was keen. There were no such birds on the mountain; starlings and English sparrows are non-native, urban birds, perfectly at home with man. They enjoy the reputation of unscrupulously taking over and driving out native wildlife species from their habitat. A person can handily predict how close he is to human habitation by noting the reduction of native species and the increase of starlings and English sparrows. Like the ubiquitous Norway rat, the pigeon, and the house mouse, starlings and English sparrows respond most favorably when natural habitats disappear parcel by parcel because of urban sprawl.

In contrast, native species are at a loss when natural conditions become scarce; they become trapped within limited pockets of available habitat, unable to migrate to more hospitable natural areas, and, unfortunately, faced with local extinction. Larger species—native hawks, falcons, owls, and large woodpeckers—those with more specialized requirements, disappear first. The rest follow. But the non-native species, like the starlings, readily migrate from other urban areas to the places vacated by the evicted native species.

I thought again of Chimney Rock and the falcons and the myriad wildlife forms indigenous to the mountain. It all boiled down to one thing: wildlife is its habitat. The two cannot be separated. Because all wild animals have specific requirements for food, cover, and places to breed, if these needs are not met, the species cannot survive for long. Suitable habitat must be considered in managing any species, or else in our future, there will only be starlings and English sparrows, rats and pigeons, and more and more and more of them.

"May I have a word with you?"

I looked up to face the blonde secretary, who stood at the restroom door. Twitching long fingers, she motioned for me to step with her into the lobby. Resting the cumbersome jug on the floor, I had hardly walked two steps from the restroom when she exclaimed in a resonant voice, "How can you justify to yourself what you're doing?"

"Pardon?"

"I'll say it again," she said more distinctly, "how can you possibly justify shutting down and locking up a wealth of archeological treasures?"

She tossed her hair back from her face as if to punctuate the question.

"You mean the ruins?"

"Yes."

"But I'm . . . we're not locking them up. I mean, not forever. And they're not being disturbed."

"I used to work on an archeological team. What you're doing is keeping all those ruins shut away from scientific investigation. Just for a couple of birds."

"But nothing's going to happen to the ruins; they'll still be there after these studies are over. Half the year the area is open to everyone; the birds migrate south."

"How would you like to sit on the snow and dig around rocks when it's zero degrees out?"

"I understand, but—"

"No. I don't think so. There's a wealth of knowledge just sitting up there for interested people to study, people who want to unravel important mysteries, and you're locking them out."

"Not permanently. The birds are endangered."

"If they're so endangered, why don't you catch them and put them in a zoo for protection? And if you can't do that, there are plenty of other good places besides Chimney Rock for those birds. If you shoo them away from here, they'll find somewhere else."

"It's not that simple."

Pausing, she ran her hands to smooth her skirt again, then looked up.

"Look, I like animals. I've watched birds before. But it really irritates me that all of those ruins are just sitting there, rotting away, while you keep people out because two birds have chosen to nest on the Rock."

I strained to keep cool. "There are only five pairs of peregrine falcons left in Colorado," I began in defense. "Not a single pair is left east of the Mississippi River. For that reason, I think it's justifiable to shut down archeological studies and intensive tourism for the few months the peregrines nest on the Rock."

"And I think you should have your birds pack their bags and move to Wyoming."

People were coming out of their offices and starting to stare. "But how can you put a price tag on an endangered species?" I asked, trying to hush my voice. "How can you say what is worth more: tourism, archeological studies, or an endangered species?"

"I'll tell you who could put a price tag on those birds. Just talk to anybody in this town and ask them what they think those birds are worth. Are they worth shutting down the million-dollar development that so many people have spent years in planning? Are they worth the thousands of dollars the local businessmen will lose if the tourist attraction doesn't go through?"

"I can understand your feelings."

"No. You don't. That's obvious."

I could feel sweat beading across my hairline. The room was stifling. She continued, "I think this whole idea of endangered species is just fine in areas where no one is going to be hurt by locking up land to keep the animals happy. But when you value a couple of birds more than people or enterprises that would benefit people, I think you're going too far."

"I don't value birds more than people—I think people need birds like peregrine falcons just as much as they need a tourist center."

"Well, I don't. Who is going to see those birds anyway? Millions of people could benefit from opening this area to tourism. Only a few bird watchers, like yourself, are going to benefit from closing off an area for the sake of a pair of falcons."

"I wish I could help you see what I'm trying to say—"

"I can see what you're saying. You're for keeping people out so you can enjoy the area for yourself."

"That isn't true!"

"Then why don't you suggest opening up the area, and see what happens to those falcons? If they leave, fine, we didn't want them anyway. I'm speaking of the people who live here and have to have jobs to be able to feed their families. But maybe you wouldn't understand that. You're only a visitor."

"I can see your point, but I think I can explain—"

"No need to explain. What you're trying to do is all right in theory, but it just doesn't work in reality. Two birds aren't worth it when you're talking in terms of millions of dollars. And also, if you're being so self-righteous, why don't you give the land back to the Indians? There's a big drive currently to give Chimney back to the Utes. It's theirs anyway. They would know what to do with the falcons. Shoot them for their feathers."

"The Utes are trying to acquire Chimney Rock?"

"You bet they are, but they won't get it; and neither will you. Maybe it's because you're young and idealistic, but let me tell you, there's more to life than birds."

I sighed, knowing it was useless to argue with her. She spoke again, confidently and without emotion.

"Think about it. Think about what you're doing. And then, when you've come to the only conclusion you can rightfully come to, I'll let you know of a good zoo for those birds, where people, lots of people, can enjoy them."

Standing very straight, she promenaded across the waiting room, cool with assurance, her straight, long blonde hair swaying behind her as she breezed behind her desk.

"Oh Marcy," she said, "don't forget your water."

Chapter Seven

 OVER THE NEXT several days, I learned the truth about living entirely alone without another human being for company and discovered I was really far more sociable than I thought. I came face to face with the fact that being outdoors without a single luxury was not quite as romantic as I had always envisioned. "Real" life in the mountains is thunderstorms, gnats, mosquitoes, flying ants, and temperatures reaching 104 degrees on the baking exposed cliffs. Life is dust, grime, and never having your hair clean or clothes fresh or any reason to put on make-up (if I had worn it, which I didn't then). It is spending everyday in hiking boots, having pants wear out in the seat from sitting too long at an observation post, a stiff neck and shoulders from being glued to a spotting scope, and no one to rub them. Life also is avoiding rattlesnakes, ticks, and black widow spiders and having cuts on the hands and bruises on the legs and torso from falling down on the rocks when exploring new places. There is no telephone to call anyone, no daily mail to break up the routine, and no fresh food.

But life in the wilderness is other things too: nights almost too bright for sleeping because of innumerable stars, time to unwind, to slough off anything not absolutely essential, a sort of shedding of skin to feel a free new creation emerge. It is time to enjoy a sunset, to sit back and laugh at the antics of a badger careening on the hillside below, to watch deer become less afraid of you as your presence becomes more familiar. Life as a field biologist is the opportunity to get to know, really know, a species other than your own. And at last, you have something that no one seems to have anymore: time to appreciate and time to think.

Just now I was sitting huddled and safe in the stuffy trailer, escaping a lightning storm and blessing Mr. Fitch. The workmen hadn't been joking. The days of early June had a clear pattern to them: crisp and gentle in the early morning, growing hotter by the hour until noon, when the wild creatures would grow steadily more quiet (and I wished I was a lizard and could crawl under a rock and go to sleep too), with a buildup of great thunderclouds by two, and then, the unleashing rain, sometimes hail, and lightning. The top of the mountain was a dangerous place in a thunderstorm. It acted like a lightning rod for its surroundings, drawing bolts to its lone crown from miles around. Once, I waited a few minutes too long before I sought the shelter of the trailer, and dashing the last mile, I observed my hair standing straight on end in air so violently charged with electricity that it audibly snapped.

It was debatable what was worse—lightning or gnats. Of course, there was nothing dangerous about gnats, but the swarming creatures ever nibbling your war-torn scalp, your arms, your legs, your face, tested what remained of your sanity; for insect repellent never seemed to work against them, and their infinitesimal bites packed an uncontrollable itch. Presently, my face and hairline were covered with little yellow scabs, and I was coerced into wearing two bandanas as an armament against them. One I wrapped tightly about my hair and another around my face, making me resemble a common bandit. If the workmen had surprised me now, I was certain the word around the Forest Service would be that the "bird lady" had gone completely off her rocker.

With no one for company, I found I often dwelled on the secretary's caustic remarks; they had a sort of sting to them that was troublesome, probably because they held a good deal of truth. The whole question had to be examined thoroughly and without emotion, for if it wasn't, her outrage about a pair of birds potentially closing off archeological studies and shutting down a multi-million dollar development had a good deal of validity.

I wondered what the ancient Anasazi would have wanted. Their presence was a growing reality for me as I lived and moved among the decaying pithouses and sandstone kivas. These "Ancient Ones," rising out of a semi-nomadic hunting and gathering culture in the first centuries B.C., settled into a remarkable and complex village and farming life that reached levels unheard of elsewhere. The earliest Anasazi, from 200 B.C. to A.D. 700, were known as the Basketmakers, a reflection of their handcrafted, beautifully woven baskets of yucca and milkweed, which they used for bowls, backpacks, water jugs, mats, string nets, and snares. The Basketmakers were dependent on horticulture—primarily the cultivation of yellow-flint corn, beans, and squash—and lived in caves or pithouses, where domestic activities and family ceremonies were held.

Around A.D. 500, these early Anasazi began making pottery and building "kivas," circular, subterranean structures where formalized ceremonies were held. They were a fair-skinned and attractive people, short and stocky in stature, with long faces and large bones. By A.D. 700, their culture began a dramatic advancement, with the crude pithouses generally being abandoned—except for kivas which were reserved for elaborate religious ceremonies—in favor of above-ground stone and masonry houses called pueblos. The Anasazi now entered their "Pueblo Period," and from A.D. 900–1100, the era of Chimney Rock habitation, their influence spread across the entire Southwest, reaching as far as Texas and Nevada. Large, vital population centers arose along the San Juan River and its tributaries. During this era, they began constructing some of their most impressive dwellings, by 1200 taking decorative arts, pottery, and architecture to then unsurpassed heights. Working with sandstone, wood, and adobe, the Anasazi exhibited brilliant artistry, combining their knowledge of materials with the skill in configuring them to the natural landscape, examples of which are displayed in the multi-storied pueblos of Chaco Canyon and the cliff dwellings of Mesa Verde.

Some communal villages had structures numbering hundreds of rooms, each single room serving to house an entire family. Kivas of fine stone craftsmanship continued to be built mostly underground—arranged in front of the houses—and were the ceremonial centers of the male Anasazi's life (women were usually forbidden inside, unless included for a specific ceremony). A woman's place in Anasazi culture, however, was not to be denigrated; they held considerable influence. The Anasazi were probably a matrilineal people, tracing their history through their mothers, not fathers. The home was "owned" by the wife, and her family made all significant decisions.

Just prior to the fourteenth century, the Anasazi mysteriously began leaving their homes. Resources were being overused and depleted; a prolonged drought and shorter, colder growing seasons forced them from their villages. By 1300, they had disappeared. Over time their culture eroded and van-

ished. Today, it is believed that their successors are the Pueblo
Indians inhabiting New Mexico and Arizona.

Although these ancient Indians had been gone from Chimney Rock for almost a millennium, they seemed to haunt every
path I travelled. Barry Layne had once remarked that a local
Indian on the Ute Tribal Council believed that the Anasazi
revered Chimney Rock and included the giant rock and, to
some extent, the falcons as part of their worship. The largest
ceremonial kiva on the mountain, measuring nearly twenty-
five feet in diameter, was positioned just below my lookout;
its opening faced the Rock and the peregrine eyrie. I felt that
peregrines, well-known for their tenacity in returning to a specific nest site for generations, had probably nested on Chimney
Rock since antiquity and during the Anasazi's reign. And
somehow I knew too, though I couldn't explain it, that the
old Indians who had lived here would have hated to see the
demise of this bird as much as I.

Of course, the secretary wouldn't agree. And she was hardly
alone. Until only recently, most people felt exactly as she did.
In the 1920's and 1930's, hawks and owls were classified as
vermin, with bounties on their heads or, rather, feet. Public
dollars had been appropriated to buy parts, usually feet, of
birds of prey in hopes of encouraging people to kill them. The
peregrine was especially vulnerable; because it was a bird-
eating hawk, it was considered one of the most abhorrent raptors of all.

Official policy reversed when scientists began discovering
the vast, beneficial roles that hawks played in the ecosystem.
Two of the most obvious I rolled over in my mind.

Farmers and ranchers are indebted to birds of prey because
hawks and owls eat rodents. Thousands of rodents. The total
weight of food required by a raptor population is of such enor-

mous magnitude that predation by birds of prey is an effective, inexpensive, and important biological control. In one study conducted by two well-known scientists, it was calculated that a raptor population of twenty-nine birds representing eleven species consumed an impressive twenty-eight thousand to ninety thousand prey in a single fall and winter and twenty-seven thousand to thirty-one thousand in spring and summer months. Quite a lot of rodents would otherwise have to be killed by artificial means—deadly poisons or traps—and would cost ranchers and taxpayers tens of thousands of dollars.

Secondly, hawks, being predators and therefore highest on the food chain, are some of the best indicators we have of changing environmental conditions. Because of their position at the peak of the energy pyramid, they are sensitive to any changes occurring within the ecosystem, either organically or inorganically. What happens to them—their reactions to toxic pesticides, for example—can eventually happen to us. In this way, they are watchdogs for our own health.

The rain was beginning to let up, and I shoved open the trailer door. The fresh green smell was overpowering, with a fragrance only possible after a cleansing storm. The smell of sage wafted up from far below, mingling with the scent of dried pine duff, like a wild version of crushed potpourri in the steaming moistness. Thronging pine siskins flocked about the yellow dandelions, perching precariously atop their long stems, then "riding the waves" as the wind and their weight toppled over the rain-weakened stalks.

I headed back to the lookout for one last hour of observing before dinner. Arthur, as usual, was perched on the top of Chimney Rock, apparently totally unaffected by the storm. Jenny was at the eyrie sheltering her nestlings, the cold and rain urging her to brood closely. The tiercel's feathers glistened with the reflection of the early evening sun. All peregrines love wind, and Arthur's spirit always seemed to come alive with storm. Many times I had seen him take off right into the worst of it, the heaviest rain, the fiercest gale; and somehow, amazingly, he always made it back. Perhaps he too experienced that indefinable urge, that wild feeling that can rise up in the midst of a storm, making you wish to grapple with the raging elements.

Watching Arthur, I knew with certainty that the secretary was wrong, though I'd never be able to explain that to her. It was not a question of a simple value judgment that animals are to be held in higher esteem than people. It was so vastly different than that. It was that we as human beings would somehow be made less each time a species was taken away.

Chapter Eight

MR. FITCH KEPT HIS WORD. On a broiling day in mid-June, I watched through heated binoculars as a Forest Service jeep bounced up the road to Chimney Rock, followed by what looked like a pickup truck that had been converted into something strange, with high mesh railings rising up from each side of a flatbed. After having been surprised once by visitors, I vowed not to let it happen again, so securing my gear from the wind and being careful to remove my two bandanas, I hiked down to greet whoever was coming.

The jeep arrived first, with Mr. Fitch at the helm; the pickup was out of sight. With a cursory nod in my direction, he climbed from the truck and regarded the trailer.

"Nice, very nice. A better place than a lot of folks call home. A trailer is a place of refuge, a place to find something clean and proper after a full day's work in the field. However," he put in, taking off his sunglasses, "it's still my opinion that a young lady should not be doing the things you are. Most of all, it's highly improper and abnormal that you have been living alone for so long. Even though it creates hardship to spare workmen these days, I have found you a partner.

"She's only a temporary employee of the Forest Service, though. She helped on the timber crew before."

Pausing to wipe his sunglasses with a kerchief, he checked them closely then adjusted them back on his nose. Both of us turned in the direction of a truck coughing and sputtering as if it were making its last stand while barely negotiating the final bend in the road.

"As you can see, the Forest Service believes in equipping its employees with necessary conveniences, including transportation. Our fleet is alarmingly low this summer, but I found your partner the perfect vehicle when I realized that the district had two garbage trucks. We will be inconvenienced, of course, but I've decided to spare one for your work."

A garbage truck. That explained the mesh fence around the trailer bed. The vehicle lurched to a sudden stop directly behind Mr. Fitch's jeep and out jumped an attractive girl with long tawny hair and a round, almost cherubic, face that was presently red from exertion or, possibly, humiliation. I was impressed by her clean-scrubbed appearance and perfectly pressed clothes, though I thought, with some sort of obstinate satisfaction, that none of this would last long. Immediately we fell into a staring contest as Mr. Fitch made introductions, and, as if from a long way away, I heard him mutter that her name was Alex Porter and that she had recently graduated in wildlife biology from Colorado State University.

The girl's Cupid's bow mouth turned up in a friendly way as she said "hi," but I noticed a wrinkling between her pale brows while she took in the situation.

"Three months, Mr. Fitch?" she said, eyeing me closely. "I'm a wildlife biologist, but my background isn't in peregrine falcons, you realize—"

"Alex, it doesn't matter! Marcy probably doesn't know any more than you. Do you, Marcy? You will provide companionship and watch out for each other's welfare. The conditions here are not entirely safe. Marcy could have fallen over the edge days ago and no one would have known."

(Now I could fall over the edge and someone would know.)

"Alex, come here." Walking past me, Mr. Fitch steered Alex to the ruins. How little he knows about friendship, I thought; just thrusting two people together does not guarantee they will like each other, let alone get along with impartial civility. Alex looked, well, agreeable enough, but spending three months alone together was enough to test any relationship, even a long-standing one. My fate was sealed now—I could see that—for better or for worse, and abstractly, I followed behind them, listening to Mr. Fitch's monologue and thinking that he made a laudable tour guide. He led Alex in a wide circuitous path to indicate the major kivas, with especial pride in the ones that the Forest Service had recently reconstructed. Someone had used heavy mortar to piece the sandstone blocks back together, and it stood out as a blatant and sloppy signature of poor craftsmanship. The job was not nearly as professional as the reconstruction at other sites, especially Mesa Verde, I thought; yet Mr. Fitch seemed to notice none of this and exalted the site as rivaling the greatest national park. At last he turned around and began heading back the way he had come, then for some reason changed his mind and charted a course through the piñon pines just to the north of the trailer, brushing past the compact bushy evergreens and stepping unconsciously on the delicious nuts spilling from their cones.

Instantly I stiffened. Mr. Fitch was unknowingly on a collision course with the little outhouse I had constructed for myself, which had the most unfortunate resemblance to a small Anasazi pithouse, being similar in size and shape and built of the same sandstone materials. He was still pointing out and talking about each little Anasazi artifact when he nearly fell into it.

His face flushed from pale, dusty rose to scarlet. Hands trembling, he removed his sunglasses to get a better look. Alex, stumbling up behind him, stopped to see what the problem was and laughed. Mr. Fitch's face, reflecting horror and aggravation, was now a deeper shade of crimson.

Collecting himself, he grappled with the sunglasses, trying to maneuver them into his breast pocket. Speechless, he marched back to the jeep at a sturdy clip, then turned towards me, his lips pursed.

"Need I say, let me repeat, need I say to you, Miss Cottrell, that you are on Forest Service property and have a responsibility to conduct yourself with propriety and decency. Yes, decency. There is a modicum of proper behavior for an employee of the U.S. government, and you have overstepped it."

Climbing into the jeep with astonishing agility, he threw on the ignition, and without another word, the little truck bounded forward like an unleashed dog. Watching him go, I wished suddenly I could fall through the earth, not coming out until I had reached the other side. Alex, however, came to my side, gently put her hand on my shoulder, and burst into laughter, and thus permanently sealed the bond to our friendship that has lasted to this day.

"I'm sorry, Marcy." She wiped the tears from her eyes. "The Indians never did anything like that."

There were definite bonuses to having a partner, especially one like Alex, who from the start was quick and dedicated; the spell of the peregrine captivated her at once, and she was willing to put in long, tedious hours. Now there was someone with whom to talk over ideas, someone to relieve your aching legs when they froze into one position after having been immobile for too long, and perhaps most beneficial of all, a partner allowed for a significant increase in data collection. Together, Alex and I could now work all the daylight hours, from five A.M. until nine at night, and two sets of eyes were far superior to one. Alex could watch one bird while I watched the other; if one of us lost sight of a fleeting falcon, the other probably still had it in her vision. Almost immediately, my notes improved in their thoroughness.

As a bonus, with the two of us scurrying like golden-mantled ground squirrels across the cliffs and with our 360 degree view, we could track both falcons' movements in every direction. This was especially valuable when it came to studying two things: the peregrines' hunting territories and their feeding patterns.

The peregrine is a true sportsman when it comes to its skill and technique of hunting. Having evolved into a specialized predator, it feeds almost exclusively on living birds that it strikes cleanly from the air after a headlong aerial pursuit. It lives on the surplus of the prey population and is thought by scientists to selectively remove substandard individuals. Unlike some predators, the peregrine never kills indiscriminantly, for the thrill of it, and what it does take it consumes completely, if not eating it in one meal then leaving it for another.

Peregrine falcons scout for their prey over wide-ranging distances, most often leaving early in the morning after sunup or in the hour before sunset. Hunting territories have been known to extend to twenty square miles, with a falcon travelling up to seventeen miles from the eyrie in search of prey. Of course, Alex and I lost sight of Arthur and Jenny when they had gone only a mile or two, but because we could trace the direction of where they were headed, I could speculate from my maps which natural features were luring them.

Favorite hunting areas for peregrines are riparian zones, places along streams, rivers, lakes, and marshes. Also, they will survey open meadows and grain fields, all of which are habitats usually filled with vital prey species: blackbirds, jays, flickers, robins, rock doves, meadowlarks, nutcrackers, and pigeons.

But there were many such places within the ten-mile radius surrounding the eyrie, which confused the issue. Constructing a grid with my topographic maps of the entire vicinity, I carefully went over each major area: the San Juan River to the west, Lake Chromo to the south, Pinyon Canyon to the east, Blue Lake to the north. Where were the peregrines going specifically? It was essential to find this out, for the vital hunting areas needed to be protected and maintained for the falcons; without them, protecting the eyrie itself would mean nothing. Once again that theme, that key principle, drummed in my brain: wildlife is habitat. Habitat loss is one of the critical factors causing many species, including raptors, to decline. I knew it was unrealistic to think that twenty square miles around each nest would be restricted from any development. It was up to me, and now Alex, to determine which areas were essential and which expendable.

In later years, we would have at our disposal a scientific method called radio telemetry to help provide the answers. By sewing a tiny radio transmitter onto the tail feather of a falcon, two scientists could divide up and trace the bird's movements by each plotting the bird's location from a different spot, and by triangulation, come up with the falcon's exact location at a given moment. But this year, Alex and I had no such equipment or luxury. We had to resort to cruder methods. And we came up with a perfect one.

All we needed was a second set of topo maps and a pair of walkie-talkies. Alex was reluctantly selected to go to town and ask Mr. Fitch for the items, which, to his credit, he granted without too much discussion. Our primitive scientific tools in hand, we were ready to begin. My post was at the top of the mountain, with my binoculars and a spotting scope and appropriate topographic maps glued together and divided up into eight numbered pieces of a pie: 1 for cardinal directions 0 to 45 degrees, 2 for 45 to 90 degrees, and so on until 8 for 315 to 360 degrees.

Alex's position was in the garbage truck, parked at the bottom of the mountain, with an identical map in her hand. At a word through the walkie-talkie, she was ready to go speeding off to track down the falcons, though how she managed wielding maps, looking through binoculars, screaming over the walkie-talkie, and driving all at the same time I was never quite sure. Because too much communication between us cut down Alex's reaction time and thus could ruin an expedition, we strove to keep our words to a minimum. We conversed by code, citing the direction the falcons were travelling by relating only the map-piece number, 1 through 8.

"Porter, Porter, this is Cottrell. Do you read?"

"10–4!"

"Arthur. Piece 6."

"10–4. Got him. I'm on my way."

For two weeks our experiment worked reasonably well. But there was a problem. All of our communication was transmitted over public radio waves on the Forest Service station, and over time, government officials grew steadily more perturbed as we interrupted their airspace. Not understanding our code or the reasoning behind it, they considered it gibberish.

But Alex and I, growing more confident in our abilities, used the walkie-talkies more and more. To clarify things, I began telling Alex of other birds of prey besides the falcons that were heading her direction.

"Porter, Cottrell again. Two T.V.'s flying on 6! Be sure to watch!"

T.V. was code for turkey vulture; a quite smart condensation, we prided ourselves.

However, our cleverness did us in. Mr. Fitch heard from his supervisor that we were disrupting the entire forest and making fun of the Forest Service. Fitch was furious and insisted that we turn in our walkie-talkies. This curtailed our progress considerably.

Later that week, after Alex and I both came to the same dispirited conclusion that our falcon-tracking days were limited, I went into town to get our weekly supplies. Noticing several people staring at me as I stood in the checkout line, I thought I must have forgotten to wash my face or done something equally horrible. Suddenly one older gentleman pointed his finger at me disparagingly.

"That girl there, she's one of 'em," he blared loudly. I felt I'd been caught shoplifting. "That girl and her sidekick. Why they get our good taxpayers' dollars and all they do is watch T.V. I heard it myself over the radio!"

Chapter Nine

ON JUNE 25TH, Barry Layne, chairman of the Rocky Mountain Peregrine Falcon Recovery Team, came to Chimney Rock to check the status of our peregrines. He brought with him climbing gear and a partner, Don Miller, who, like Barry, was a devoted scientist and falconer. The similarities between the two men were apparent at once. Both were tall, fit, and lean with swarthy complexions, but their greatest similarity was their utter dedication to their work. For the last decade, they had spent every spring and every summer scouring cliffs and ledges throughout the United States and Canada for signs of peregrines. During the fall and winter, they helped formulate management plans and goals to protect the few falcons that remained. As long as I had known Barry, I had never witnessed him put in less than a twelve-hour work day. But he was not alone. His devotion verging on fanaticisim was the standard for raptor biologists everywhere. Saving the last of the birds was their purpose and their goal, and Barry and Don and people like them risked much—a normal family life, a sane existence, and, at times, even their lives—for this single reason.

They had brought with them a third companion. Like a fidgeting old nanny, Don hovered over a wooden crate that held the honored guest, a three-week-old little white mound of feathers and wrinkled skin. The thing, a nestling peregrine, or eyas, was as ugly as it was pathetic, looking nothing like the sleek, royal animal who spawned it. The bird had been abandoned by its wild parents when still an egg. Barry had rescued it and placed it in an artificial incubator, where it had hatched, and for the last three weeks it had been raised in captivity.

How helpless it was! Baby raptors like this are classed as "semi-precocial," for though they hatch with their eyes open and with a sheathing of down, they are dependent for five to six weeks on their parents for food and safekeeping. Bone growth is nearly completed half way through this time, but the growth of feathers doesn't occur until the second three weeks of the nestling period, hence the creature's mangy-looking appearance.

The little bird's face looked tired and droopy and more than just slightly cross. In fact, taken together, the falcon more appropriately resembled a fractious old man than a fierce bird, but no older gentleman would have feet such as its. Little wonder that John James Audubon had called the peregrine the "great footed hawk." It sprouted such enormous yellow feet!

All the hopes of Barry and Don were pinned on this pitiful-looking thing. It symbolized the purpose of the Peregrine Falcon Recovery Team, which was to amplify, in any way possible, the declining population of peregrines. Scientists use several methods. "Nest augmentation" is the placing of nestlings, such as the one Don held, or unbroken, viable eggs in wild falcon nests with the hope that they will be accepted, hatched, and raised by wild parents. As a second technique, because there are so few peregrines left and because many of their historical eyries have been taken over by their desert cousin, the prairie falcon, biologists will sometimes add peregrine nestlings or eggs to prairie falcon nests, apparently with no ill effects.

"Captive breeding" is yet another method used to increase the population. It is based on the principle of hatching and raising birds in captivity, then either returning them to the wild in places where organochlorine pesticide residues are low enough to allow survival or keeping them in centers for further breeding purposes.

Prior to 1973, scientists attempting captive breeding of peregrines experienced only failure. The birds were too sensitive, and artificial insemination and breeding produced no results. There were predictions it could never be done. But in 1973, Dr. James Enderson of Colorado Springs, after years of intense effort, was at last successful in hatching in captivity an egg of an artificially inseminated *Falco peregrinus anatum*. Once the breakthrough had occurred, the news spread quickly worldwide, and captive breeding is now widely practiced in the United States, Canada, England, and Europe.

Today, over fourteen years after the first hatch, with further refinements and skill, dozens of peregrines are raised in captivity each year. In North America, three major centers exist for the purpose of breeding peregrines, at Cornell University, Fort Collins, Colorado, and Edmonton, Alberta. Several hundred captive-bred fledgling peregrines have been "hacked" (returned) to the wild, with a few successful individuals establishing themselves in an area to breed.

Accomplished scientists also have a fourth procedure at their disposal: retrieving thin-shelled or damaged eggs from wild nests before the eggs are injured irreparably. Once back at the breeding centers, the eggs are meticulously patched, glued, covered with a thin layer of paraffin, and placed in an artificial incubator to hatch.

"This is going to be one hell of a job," Don muttered with his usual optimism, while precisely arranging the climbing ropes and carabineers. "It's going to be a bitch to climb. And probably nothing there."

"I'm certain they have young," I put in.

"I'll believe it when I see it. Let's get moving. We want to be over, up, and back by four o'clock. Here. Carry these."

While Alex stayed behind to observe, I prepared to accompany Don and Barry to the base of Chimney Rock, where Barry would climb the seventy-five feet to the eyrie. While sheer, high cliffs like this one put climbers at a serious disadvantage, they are a boon for nesting peregrines who have evolved to select the most remote and precipitous cliffs for their eyries. The heights of acceptable cliffs vary from fifty to three hundred or more feet. Those nests closer to human habitation are more quickly abandoned if disturbed, and those with a greater degree of wilderness, like Chimney Rock, are the most desirable and occupied year after year.

Swinging on my pack, I reflected on how I had lived for nearly a month less than a quarter mile away from the peregrine eyrie, yet I had never ventured to it, for two reasons: because to do so might cause the falcons to abandon the nest (a worry that was a possibility today) and because the trail over, if it could be called by such a civilized name, traversed a knife-edge ridge that dropped off several hundred feet on both sides.

I dared not look down as I went along behind, stepping cautiously, as if tiptoeing across a balance beam. (It didn't help that I had always despised gymnastics in school, particularly the balance beam.) We made it in less than a half hour with only one minor mishap, when Barry kicked over a chunk of eroded shale that uncovered a submerged yellow-jacket nest, sending dozens of nasty hornets swarming at our feet.

Only Don was stung. At the base of the Rock, Barry swiftly draped climbing ropes around his taut body, arranged his helmet, and strapped on the carabineers, while Arthur flew furiously above us. Craning her head over to watch, Jenny stuck to the nest, never letting us out of her sight.

Barry reached up to test the firmness of the sandstone, grimacing as it crumbled in his hands.

"Great," Don moaned out loud. "What a bitch."

"I want to do this thing as quickly as possible, so be ready with the eyas when I call for it," Barry said.

I was the one responsible for the bird now, having portaged it in my backpack across the abyss. Don assisted Barry in climbing, and the two focused their complete attention on the task. Don was right, of course, this was a bad rock. A bad climb. A sense of foreboding came over me as I saw Barry grope with his sinewy arms to reach for handholds that just weren't there.

With each foot Barry gained, Arthur's defense became more agitated. He raced madly among the rocks, weaving arcs around Barry's clinging body. At times skidding over to fly upside down or twirling in midair and plunging to the earth, Arthur was the master of the atmosphere. The air bent to yield to him all authority, bowed to his slightest whim, while Barry looked wooden and sadly contorted, like a fumbling giant spider climbing an invisible web. When Barry had conquered thirty feet, it was Jenny's signal to sweep from the nest in a straight dive towards him, missing him merely by inches. The two birds were unified in their frantic force, and my mind reeled at the frenzy. Did we really have to do this—interfere with nature. Couldn't we just leave the peregrines alone? The scientist in me rationalized: Of course not; this is for their benefit. This is how we hope to save them. But the woman in me did not feel thus. I could only sympathize with the birds' torment.

Finally Barry made it safely to the nest ledge and yelled for the eyas. Taking one last peek at the wee ball of down, I strapped the precious cargo—more expensive than diamonds—onto a rope Barry had flung down. Within seconds the rope became taut, and the screeching bird was hoisted upward.

"This means there are young in the nest!" I cried delightedly, with a sly glance at Don, who merely grunted. I always suspected that Don felt a woman could never be a true raptor biologist, whatever a true raptor biologist was in his opinion.

"What's he doing now?" I asked, craning my neck.

"Reconstructing the nest ledge," Don replied.

I was aware that until young peregrines can fly, they face a constant danger of tumbling from the ledge. The threat is even more real when the nestlings are on the verge of fledging. People disturbing peregrine eyries have witnessed nestlings, out of fear, falling from the eyrie at this sensitive time and smashing on the rocks below. Barry obviously found this nest inadequately protected, and was placing rocks around the periphery of the eyrie to try to reinforce it.

He called when he was ready to begin his rappel. Don swore, and I prayed the pins Barry had secured for protection would hold in the feeble, rotting sandstone. These were the times lives were on the line, with scientists endeavoring to climb cliffs that should never be attempted in the first place.

But the pins held. Barry was down. Brown rivulets of sweat

poured from his face, and the men were grasping each other, and then me, and then slapping each other again, for the news this time was good.

"Four little healthy devils. Three weeks old about. That old tiercel's done good." Barry took a swig of water. "Stuffed the little guy in the eyrie, and they probably won't even realize it."

"Will they accept it?"

"We'll find out soon. I think so. Though that's a heavy load for one pair to care for. But they're fat and sassy youngsters, so the hunting must be good."

"How many does that make?" I asked. "Hatchlings this year, I mean."

"Speed it up," Don interrupted, "We want to get the hell out of here so things can settle down. You can gab all you want back there."

"Two, now five . . . seven total. Only one other nest besides this one has been successful this year in our region. This one is damned important."

Crossing the ridge back wasn't nearly as traumatic, for I had wings on my feet with the news we had four nestlings, and one foundling. My joy was dampened only at the thought that a scant two nests were successful this season, making for pretty atrocious statistics. After resting forty-five minutes, the biologists prepared to leave, and after a moment's hesitation, I ventured to ask Barry if he had known of the proposed tourist development and had omitted telling me.

"Oh sure I know of it; what about it?"

I said everyone seemed to be flying in all directions about it.

Barry laughed. "Forget it. You're not here to be a mediator. We'll discuss it another time. It's no big deal. What is imperative is that these five nestlings live to fledge, find mates, and reproduce in the wild. That means *no* interference of any kind with this eyrie. Do you hear me? No harassment. No viewing by so-called tourists. In fact, I don't want any people at all besides you and Alex in this vicinity until the young have fledged. These birds must be under constant surveillance."

"You understand that?" Don barked.

I nodded. Of course I did. But at the time, I hadn't a clue to what it was to mean.

Chapter Ten

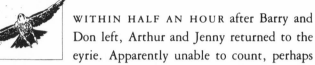 WITHIN HALF AN HOUR after Barry and
Don left, Arthur and Jenny returned to the
eyrie. Apparently unable to count, perhaps
even if they could, they accepted the little orphan without
hesitation, though it would mean far more work for them.
Over the next few days, they stepped up their pursuit of food
almost incrementally, and now, with the nestlings nearing
four weeks old, Jenny began actively hunting again. Her
efforts were sorely needed; weighing 50 percent more than
Arthur, she could take larger, bulkier items with ease, while
her mate was forced to concentrate on the smaller, more wiry
prey. The fact that the eyrie contained more than three youngsters also required the falcon to begin hunting earlier, more
frequently, traveling longer distances than it would if the
brood had only been composed of one.

The demands of the nestlings were increasing each day. A
young falcon in the second half of the nestling period consumes vast amounts of food, soon exceeding the intake of an
adult of the same sex. Each chick requires four to eight meals
per day. The parents began merely dropping off unplucked
prey in the nest in their rush to gather more food, and then,
when the youngsters were finished eating, they rushed again
to carry away the remains, to keep the ledge clean.

One thing was fortunate—the peregrine's increasing appetites were timed exactly with the peak in prey availability, which provided the maximum chance of survival for the young. This intricate balance is found throughout nature, with predator species having evolved to match their peak needs with the seasonal abundance of their prey. A further step removed, these prey species have also evolved to reach their prime in relation to the most favorable time in the annual climatic cycle.

It is an intricate strategy, beautiful in its fine-tuning and its precise workability: a system of species, such as a population of birds of prey, is dependent upon its subsystems (prey species and nesting sites), which in turn are dependent upon their subsystems (climate, geological features, range conditions). A scientist, therefore, cannot afford to study a single species without regarding those things that impinge upon it. They are all wrapped up together in a complete, tight ball.

With the young three and a half weeks old, a critical phase in the nesting cycle, Alex and I observed the falcons becoming substantially more protective of their progeny. Thus we began to concentrate on another aspect of the research: the reactions of the adult peregrines toward intruders—bird, beast, and man—when they ventured within a half-mile of the nest. The falcons vented their annoyance through several forms of communication, sometimes vocal, sometimes bodily aggressive. I was now able to recognize three distinct vocalizations that the falcons used between themselves:

A soft, guttural "echup-chup-chup-chup" was a delightful, affectionate bit of intimacy, reserved for times when the peregrines were alone together and getting along well. Because this monogamous pair had been together at least several years and had survived the unsettled period of early togetherness, we heard this often. It was as if they were saying everything was all right with their world; at these times, I too derived a vicarious sense of the contentment they shared.

A second type of communication was evident when the falcons were mildly distressed over something, which was usually not too serious but still cause for alertness. Either Arthur or Jenny, usually Jenny, would scratch out a long, piercing wail, sounding something like a cat with its tail caught in a door. If the reason for the disturbance abated, the wailing would soon cease, but if not and the falcons perceived what they considered a real danger, they would then break out into their third form of communication, a fierce, throaty, and disturbingly beautiful cry: "Kak-Kak-Kak."

This was the call of the peregrine. It is a call that forever will haunt me, even when I am hundreds of miles away from them. It is the peregrines' statement and their identity; if a wail is a war chant, this symbolizes active battle. Usually it signifies that a golden eagle, great horned owl, or man is somewhere within a mile or less of the eyrie. A wild peregrine will tolerate none of these intruders, and if the danger continues to edge nearer, the vocal and aerial battle of the peregrine will increase in intensity, as we had witnessed when Barry had climbed to the nest.

Because science demands relative objectivity in recording data (actually "science" doesn't demand it, scientists do, and though they pretend to achieve it, it is a rare scientist who doesn't let his own past history, biases, and previous training impinge on his objective view of the data he is gathering), Alex and I devised a method to quantify the degree of the peregrine's sensitivity to intruders:

o = No show of defense
1 = Mildly disturbed; wailing
2 = Wailing and some kakking, or one stoop (defense short-lived)
3 = Kakking, flying about, ten minutes or less
4 = Kakking and stooping continuously while disturber in view
5 = Kakking, stooping, full-fledged defense, lasting for an hour or more, even if intruder is hidden from view

After several weeks, we became quite proficient at guessing what was bugging the birds from their visible, communicated reaction. "That's got to be a raven," Alex would say, when Jenny would pull a 2. "Aha! A Buteo hawk," I'd cry, when they'd begin acting 4. These were proud moments.

But times did arise when Arthur or Jenny created a stir for no reason we could see; usually we'd let these pass, thinking they were of no great consequence. But, as we were to learn by default, Arthur and Jenny were far better than any highly trained watchdog when it came to their reaction number 5. Indeed, when this flag was raised, it meant trouble, no denying it, and we had to act fast to see what the problem was. On a day in late June, we could detect no golden eagle or horned owl that was vexing them, but both birds were reacting violently to something. Which could mean only one thing—man.

"Cripe, who's coming now?" Alex sighed, pinning her vision on a station wagon lugging up the road. "This is such a pain. What the devil is the problem with Mr. Fitch?"

Mr. Fitch had repeatedly promised to erect "area-closed" signs at the base of the road. Even though our Chimney Rock road was locked with a Forest Service gate (and I knew just how good that method of security was), people seemed to show up from out of nowhere every few days, primarily wilderness hikers making the walk for the view. So far, luckily, they all had been amenable when either Alex or I would greet them with the news that they couldn't stay, using the feeble excuse that the Colorado Division of Wildlife was conducting a closed study on ravens. (This was Barry Layne's brainchild.) We had radioed Mr. Fitch over and over again to tell him that we were being interrupted, and to ask him politely where his promised signs were, only to get his automatic response that he was "working on it."

"I'll go down, Alex," I volunteered, tiredly.

One thing I had learned this summer was that a person should refrain from volunteering for anything. Arriving at the base camp, I saw a weighted-down station wagon, trudging like a pregnant woman nearing imminent delivery, bearing nine people, all sitting hot, cramped, and bunched up together. Wanting to strangle Fitch, I tried to put on a happy smile and strolled to the driver's window. Out popped a man's head; I couldn't actually see his eyes because they were shaded behind sunglasses, but I could feel antagonism emanating from them. No, this time would not be like the others.

"Hi. Quite a road, isn't it?"

The man remained quiet. Thrusting open the door and clambering out, he stretched to a forbidding, 6 1/2′ height, stopping to take a deep breath that inflated his barrel chest. I shuddered, then fell into my recorded soliloquy on the "ravens."

"What do you mean, closed?" he asked.

I began explaining again. "I see," he said coolly. His silver hair was backlighted with a rim of light, resembling a halo, and his height advantage made me feel as if he were looking at me from a great distance. I felt about as large and significant as a land snail.

The man clapped his hands. "Okeydokey folks. Let's get moving. This is it."

Hadn't he heard me? "I'm sorry, but this area is off limits."

Removing the sunglasses, he frowned. "Pardon me. These," he made a sweeping gesture, "these are my guests. Need I explain we have driven since eight o'clock this morning from New Mexico for a picnic. A picnic is to be held here. Now run along, missy, will you please?"

Pulling myself to my full 5'9", I attempted to look him squarely in the eyes. "Sir, it's impossible for you to have your picnic here."

"Must I add we are all tired and impatient after such an arduous excursion?"

"I'm sorry, really I am, but the area is off limits to all visitors for the next several months. There will be signs. The district ranger—"

"—Fitch, yes, I know him well."

"Mr. Fitch is putting up some signs—"

The man glanced at his shoes—white, patent dress ones—and, with well-practiced aptitude, brushed the blowing dust from them by rubbing them on the backside of each pant leg. "What school are you from, missy?"

"School? I'm not a student. I'm a biologist; I work for the Colorado Division of Wildlife."

"Well, what do you know. What do you know. I, too, am from the Colorado Division of Wildlife. I'm Maurice Richards."

I had never heard of the man. Well, I thought, relieved, at least I could tell the truth now. He must know Barry, must have heard mention of the peregrine work and the girl hired to conduct it. The crisis was over. Extending my hand, I explained to him who I was.

"I knew you'd come to your senses. Now, if you'll excuse us, we have a picnic to attend to."

"Oh yes, your picnic! I can recommend some lovely spots near here. There's a beautiful overlook on Hermosa Mountain, which is just north of here, or perhaps if you'd prefer being by a lake, Blue Lake is pristine and wonderfully secluded. If you have a map with you, I can direct you how to get there—"

"You don't seem to be reading me. We're having our picnic here. Right here. Right now. Are you deaf?"

"Pardon—?"

"I said, are you deaf? I have told you three times that we have come here for expressly one purpose, our picnic. And we are going to have our picnic, now, with or without your permission. Please, move aside."

Three grim-faced perspiring men and five bewildered women were caught propped half way in and out of the car, unsure how to proceed. Maurice Richards waved his hand, gesturing for them to follow.

"What's that bird, Maurice?" asked one of the ladies in a whimpering voice. "The one up there, flying like that?" I could have told her it was Arthur and that he was flying like that because she was disturbing him and that, if these people continued this folly, all hell might break loose at this eyrie, because two such major disturbances in less than a week were two too many, especially considering the added dimension of the fifth nestling.

"You cannot have your picnic here," I said miserably. "I regret all your trouble, but that's all there is to it."

"I cannot believe what I'm hearing."

"I said you can't stay here any longer."

The rage in his voice ascended an octave higher. "Are you looking to be fired?"

"Mr. Richards, please, you've had a long trip and I've disappointed you. But there is no way you can take all of these people to the observation point. The peregrines have been through enough. I hope you can understand."

"I sure can understand one thing: you will not be under my employ any longer than it takes me to get to a telephone and tell Layne of your conduct. This is absolutely inexcusable."

"Well, do as you must." I sighed.

"You are impertinent, discourteous, and . . . and an utter idiot. Don't you know who I am? The power I have?"

"No."

"Well I am not going to stand here to be insulted by you any longer!"

He turned back to face his guests with an ingratiating smile. "My friends, we seem to have encountered a small problem. I have decided that our picnic would be far more enjoyable at a lovely place I know of on Hermosa Mountain, forty-five minutes from here. The view far surpasses this. So if you'll climb back in the car." Still smiling, he spat from under his breath, "As for you, young lady, you are not and will never be a biologist. I will see to that personally."

I groaned; another friend won. How many did this make? At times like this, Colorado Springs, college, and all I had left behind seemed a far more rational existence. But could I go back now? No, and I didn't want to; the person I was then was behind me already—too far behind to recapture her.

"What the hell is going on down there?" Barry howled over

the phone. "You've got one of our highest officials as mad as a hornet; it's all I can do to personally keep him from having you deported."

"Barry," I coughed agonizingly. "He wanted a picnic."

"A what?"

I sighed, and began explaining. Fitch was hovering over my shoulder, wearing a dog-faced expression—hands fidgeting nervously behind him—after having called me in, chastising me publicly on the radio. This was all too much.

Suddenly Barry laughed out loud. "I've been dying for days to hear this story. Grand! Grand!! Richards's an ass."

And I, I was not fired; I think to the secret disappointment of Mr. Fitch.

Chapter Eleven

 WHEN TRAGEDY STRIKES, everyone is
somehow made alone to deal with the cir-
cumstances. Each person must rely on his
own amassed, inner resources to cope in the best way he
knows. Scientists have often disputed whether animals feel
such things as grief and suffering, such as when a beloved
master goes away or a mate dies. Some researchers believe that
animals feel little or no emotions at all. I do not agree with
them. From what I experienced my first summer at Chimney
Rock, I can never again glibly doubt that an animal, even a
mere bird, has the ability to suffer complex feelings such as
disorientation, grief, and loneliness at the death of a life's
mate. To those scientists who do not agree with me, all I can
say is they were not there; they did not see the things Alex
and I did, nor witness the repercussions.

On June 29, a bizarre glitch became apparent in our data.
The observation sheet I held in my hand looked disturbingly
unlike the other dozens of red and blue crisscrossed pages that
had been amassing since early June. This white sheet of paper
consisted only of simple, sporadic blue lines, which meant that
only one peregrine had been spotted all day—the tiercel,
Arthur. For some reason, Alex and I had both missed observing Jenny. But her stops were brief at the eyrie these days; she
was intensely involved in hunting for the fast-growing nest-

lings, an explanation that seemed perfectly adequate and squelched my alarm. Hunting was a demanding mistress; she would be back.

But when a second day passed and the notes showed only blue scribblings, never red, my apprehension mounted. Of course we were making errors someplace. We obviously were overlooking the slinking falcon when she darted to and from the nest, but, then again, that thought was ridiculous. The tiercel maybe could slip away unnoticed by us now and then, but never Jenny, who was ostentatious in everything she did, whether it was heralding her return from a successful hunt or molesting the poor, martyred ravens. Jenny never slinked.

Three days after we had last seen Jenny, on the afternoon of July 1, an event occurred that forced me to the depressing conclusion that something was indeed going haywire; it was not merely the result of our inadequate powers of observation.

Arthur, the steady, predictable tiercel, was acting peculiar. Alex and I had been watching him closely to notice any change in behavior that might provide a clue to the unusual circumstances, and our notes confirmed that he was spending much more time at the Rock than ever before. For hour-long stretches he perched alone by the eyrie, something he never did before, seemingly waiting for an event to happen. Unfortunately, as a consequence of his sedentary behavior, he was hunting less than normal, and the few times during the day when he did hunt and return to Chimney Rock with prey dangling in his talons, his standard cry for Jenny to retrieve it in the usual "food exchange" manner yielded no results. This seemed to distress him. After feeding the nestlings, he then returned to his placid existence of sitting next to the eyrie, moving little, and waiting.

At four o'clock in the afternoon, Arthur's calm behavior took a radical leap. Arriving home from a hunt (another unsuccessful one), he called out for his mate. There was no response. Arthur glided to the nest, looked in, and echupped. Nothing. Suddenly he catapulted to the base of the Rock, twisted 180 degrees to soar a hundred feet up above the nest, and, flying like an aerobatic plane with a madman pilot at the controls, snap-rolled several times, slowly unwinding to artfully land on the crest of the Rock.

Once situated, Arthur again called out the gentle, almost tender "echup, chup" to his mate. Waiting patiently, he turned his black, regal head to scan all directions unfolding below him. But only the wind sighed a response. Arthur called again, "echup, chup, chup." There remained only silence.

His feathers spread wide, the bird ran a thorny talon through them. Sitting erect, he shook himself. The feathers spread out again, he turned his face upward, closing his body tight and rigid. The peregrine falcon opened his beak and emitted a cry like the screeching moan of a wounded animal, the cry of a creature in suffering. The sound lanced through the air to reverberate off the hot rocks and shale slopes below. The sadness in the outcry was unmistakable; having heard it, I will never doubt that an animal can suffer emotions that we humans think belong to our species alone.

Arthur's behavior changed after the outburst. For the remainder of the day, and for a full day hence, he refused to leave the Rock. He did not hunt, nor eat. Unmoving, he made a forlorn statue on the cliff when the sun rose in the morning, a lifeless taxidermy specimen when it set in the evening.

Alex and I were deeply alarmed. If Jenny were indeed gone, Arthur presumably would find no replacement for her next year. The Chimney Rock eyrie would face the dismaying fate of so many other wild peregrine eyries: it would be abandoned. In addition, and far more urgent, if Arthur continued with this peculiar behavior and refused to hunt again soon, the five nestlings surely had no chance of survival.

Regretfully, I knew the inevitable call had to be made to Barry Layne, and this I dreaded. I had no answers. What had caused this tragic twist of events? Whatever had happened to Jenny?

On Monday I left Alex to carry on and drove to the Lost Canyon Cafe to place my call. As I shut the gate to our mountain road, the snap of the lock rang with finality.

The Lost Canyon Cafe was the closest place with a phone; I went there often to refill the water jugs, as it was far less hassle than driving all the way into town to the Forest Service, but the problem was that the phone was on center stage in the restaurant, hanging from a wall near the middle of the room, which insured that any kind of private conversation was virtually impossible. The art of eavesdropping had become something of an attraction for isolated farmers and ranchers who stopped here to confab and drink a pot of coffee. If you whispered your conversation, you only made matters worse, setting off an alarm that something of importance was being relayed.

I reached Barry Layne at once. To my bitter news, he responded that he hoped I was mistaken, then slammed down the phone. In my mind, this sealed the eyrie's fate. I wanted to slump with sadness, but now all the faces in the diner were turned towards me; so I faked a smile of confidence. From the corner of my eye I saw Edna Lowrie, the cafe's owner, marching over to me, with a questioning look on her face.

Several times before I had talked with her briefly, coming

to the conclusion early on that she was the one in charge around these parts. Over time she would become one of the peregrines' greatest supporters and a deep, personal friend to both Alex and me, but until she decided your worth, she could be intimidating. Many folks were chary of her tongue, for she spoke life as she saw it, without any hesitancy or pretense, a trait that would come to our aid many times in the upcoming months and years.

Edna clutched her fingers about my arm. "Saw you standing over there at the phone. Join me for a cup of coffee?"

Before I could answer, I was led to her table, which was strategically positioned two tables away from the kitchen, where she could oversee everything. Seating herself, she pulled out a cigarette and motioned for the waitress to bring us coffee. With a quick sweep of her arm, she dusted the crumbs off the red-checked tablecloth and plopped her elbows down resolutely, cupping her face, which was framed by wispy, brown hair streaked with gray, and regarding me unabashedly. Soon, she relaxed, then smiled an unusual half smile that only lifted up the corners of her mouth, not affecting her heavy-lidded eyes, which stayed steady and cool.

"You know, I think they are wrong, what they're saying about you," she said. "It makes me realize that those jokers on the road crew are just a bunch of dumbos."

"Road crew? I don't know anyone on a road crew."

She yawned and put down her cigarette. "Oh, you're wrong. Actually you're a favorite topic of theirs."

The waitress slowly put down two cups of coffee, then lingered, humming to herself.

"I've been watching you and Alex. You're not gold bricks, or all the rest of those maligning things they say about you. I think you're doing something because you believe in it. Am I right?"

The waitress could contain herself no longer and dropped the coffee pot on the table. "Oh, tell her the rest, Edna!"

"Fern, get lost."

"But you're not telling the half of it." She turned to face me. "You should have been in here an hour ago. Edna's a real lion when something makes her mad. And what those guys were saying about you did it. She told them to shut their mouths, take their damn boots off the table, and not to come back anymore."

"That's enough, Fern."

The coffee was tasting worse every moment.

"Like I said, some martyr has to do what you're doing," Edna put in. "I like those falcons. From all I know they never hurt anybody, though the way folks carry on around here you'd think they carried the plague."

"Really, I should go, Edna. Alex will be wondering about me."

"Sit down. I'm not through. I have something else I want to talk to you about. Did I overhear right that lately you haven't seen one of the falcons?

"Well, is it true?"

My attempt to remain calm was belied by an unsteady grip on the coffee cup. "Um, yes. Yes it is."

"I knew it! Fern. Rag over here. The girl spilled." Over rushed Fern, taking lengthy pains to clean up the mess. "Well, that's too bad," Edna went on. "Darn rotten shame. You see, I live in a farmhouse up Pinyon Canyon. A quarter mile or so down the road from our house is a telephone pole where one of your falcons always sat. I'd see it almost every day.

"I know what a falcon is," she said emphatically, seeing my skepticism. "A big bird with a black head, real showy. It was usually there in the morning when I'd leave for work. Looking for gophers, I suppose . . . Other folks saw it too."

The story was plausible. One of the places we had frequently traced Jenny heading was Pinyon Canyon, though neither Alex nor I ever knew exactly where she went once she got there.

The stub of her cigarette was squashed out, and Edna started on a new one. "Just lately I haven't seen it anymore. And after what you just said, I know now I'm right saying it was shot."

"Shot?"

"Yeah. Somebody killed it. Too many people knew it was there. And then, of course, the feathers."

"What do you mean?"

"Long ones. The feathers were scattered all around the base of that pole one morning. Funny thing though, I thought of picking them up, and I should have done it. I could kick myself now. When I got home that night, they were gone. The place had been gone over clean."

I felt myself growing rigid. "What day was it you think you saw those feathers?"

"Think? I saw them, plain as day. And I've never seen the bird again since. Let's see, it was last Wednesday. No, couldn't have been. Didn't go to work Wednesday. Tuesday. It was Tuesday the twenty-ninth."

I gritted my teeth. The date was right.

"These dumbheads around here can't ever leave well enough alone. They don't know what they want. A tourist center isn't going to make us rich; it'll only make the developers rich. And the one thing I hate more than the government is developers.

"Fern, for God's sake, go get this girl some more coffee!" The waitress fled. "Just look at her," she bellowed. "She's all worn out."

She reached out and put a hand on my shoulder. "Well, cheer up. Don't feel so bad. Look on the bright side. There's always a bright side, though just now I can't think of what it is."

Edna smiled sympathetically. "Well now, how about a hamburger?"

Chapter Twelve

 FOR THE REMAINDER of the afternoon and the day following, I combed Pinyon Canyon looking for any hint of a bird or feathers or a carcass, but I found nothing to verify Edna's story. Or, for that matter, to disprove it. The only certainty was that Jenny never returned.

I disliked considering that many local residents would rejoice at the failure of this eyrie, but with Jenny gone and the young starving and needing care, it seemed the likely conclusion. The only thing that could possibly save the eyrie was if Arthur suddenly began filling the roles of both mother and father, but that possibility seemed remote. Renowned scientist Tom Cade has estimated that during a single nesting period an average pair of adult peregrines and their nestlings require for subsistence at least fifty-four thousand grams of food, which in graphic terms means two thousand medium-sized songbirds. That quantity required two birds hunting. No, one bird could not do it alone.

The situation at Chimney Rock seemed hopeless; thoughts tumbled through my mind like unwanted guests. Chalk up one more species for extinction, I mused gloomily. Yet consider the repercussions. Author/scientist Paul Ehrlich has said that each time a species becomes extinct it is like popping rivets from an airplane. The plane will stay aloft at first, but eventually it is unable to fly and will crash. In other words, man can survive with many fewer species on earth, but sometime, even our species will be at risk. Scientist George Schaller put our skewed values more succinctly when he noted how peculiar it is that people think nothing of giving millions of dollars for a wing in an art museum for their posterity even though paintings can be reproduced. If a species is wiped out, it can never be replaced.

Alex and I saw to our dismay that the ravens were having a heyday with Jenny gone. Arthur didn't seem to mind, and, what was worse, he didn't chase away the turkey vultures, those specters of death that for the last several days had been circling ominously above the Rock. Once they had swept directly past the eyrie. This seemed only to punctuate the outcome I knew was inevitable.

I woke up depressed on the mornings following my visit to the cafe. Jenny had now been gone for four days. Arthur still sat glued to the Rock, but I knew the end was near; he would be leaving soon. The breakfast oatmeal tasted stale in the morning, and Alex and I trudged heavyhearted to the lookout, wondering how much longer we would be here. On the fifth morning of Jenny's absence, Arthur was already gone. Well, it had happened. Arthur had abandoned the cliff sometime in the night. Now it was over. The spotting scope needn't be unpacked. I'd return it to Colorado College and look for a new job and leave this disagreeable place with its disagreeable people.

"Look! There he is!" Alex cried. "He's bringing in prey! Food for the nestlings!"

So began one of the strangest episodes in the history of Chimney Rock, perhaps of the bird kingdom. Something like a catharsis had occurred overnight in the male peregrine, transforming his behavior. A new vitality empowered everything about him, a new determination and purpose. With perseverance such as I had never before or since witnessed in any animal, Arthur began hunting and providing for his nestlings. For the next week and the one after, the single bird became as three. Never stopping to rest, to preen his feathers and stretch, to doze as he once did in the hottest part of the day, Arthur hunted with almost palpable intensity. At 5:00 A.M. he was gone. When he returned to the eyrie with food, he lit only for the instant it took to drop it off, then swept off again. Arthur worked unceasingly from dawn till dusk.

As far as I know, this remarkable devotion to duty when a male bird is suddenly left alone without his mate midstream in the nestling cycle is unheard of in most species of birds or at least exceedingly rare, and for Arthur it did not let up until long after the nestlings had fledged. The notes we took resembled electrocardiograms with their frantic intensity; for the next several days, I was not exactly sure what was coming or going, yet the thrill in knowing that Arthur was not defeated, that the Chimney Rock eyrie still had a chance, superseded all my thoughts.

I will always enjoy contrasting those days to my subsequent years at Chimney Rock, when Arthur was indeed fortunate to attract a new mate and raise new clutches of nestlings, for during later years he never put in a fraction of the hours he did during the summer of Jenny's death. In fact, Arthur generally left the bulk of the hard work to his new and vigorous mate, while he rested, preened, and slept. I suppose, however, after what he did, he deserved it.

Seven days had elapsed since Jenny's absence when Barry Layne returned to Chimney Rock, once again accompanied by Don Miller, to reclimb the rock and investigate the status of the nest. Accompanying the two men was a third gentleman, the local wildlife conservation officer of the region, Pat Waters. Tall and lean and fit, with blue and youthful eyes surrounded by dozens of smile lines, Pat at fifty years old looked an old-fashioned cowboy far more than a government official, and his laconic and genteel ways only verified it. Pat Waters would come into our lives and to our defense many times during our stay at Chimney Rock, but today he brought only a $1500 police radio for our use, at the same time stressing the need for its safekeeping.

"Let's get this over with before the tiercel gets back," Don said, stone faced.

Because Barry had left well-secured pins in the rock from his last climb, the ordeal took half the time and effort. Barry and Don were up, down, and back at our lookout in less than an hour, their dark faces revealing what they had uncovered even before they'd caught their breath to relate the story.

In his big hands Barry held the decomposing remains of three nestling peregrine falcons. They had starved, probably within the first three days, and the sight of the feeble bodies was wrenching, exacerbated by the thought that we had lost four peregrines at a time when only a handful remained in the wild. Within each of us was a sadness that none of us expressed. I envisioned, as I had dozens of times before, a future when the cliffs and canyons would never again hear the whoosh of a peregrine's stoop or the refrain of a peregrine's cry.

"What about the other two?" asked Pat. "Dead?"

"Dead?" Barry suddenly lit up. "Anything but. Those two friggin' little buggers wouldn't stop nipping my fingers the whole time I was fooling around—some pretty mean swipes, too. They'll be okay. They're what we've got to put our faith in, if this eyrie's to make it."

Barry, Don, and Pat left that night, and once more it was just Alex and I, Arthur, and the two nestlings at the cliff. A new emptiness wafted in the air, and for the first time I felt a surge of loneliness, a desire for the company of people. Lots of them. Alex fell to sleep after dinner, leaving me alone with the yipping coyotes. The galaxy of cold stars piercing the black above me seemed to amplify my sense of isolation. But I reminded myself that Barry was right. We were lucky; we still had two nestlings, and an active eyrie. And Arthur. We must put our faith in these.

Of course we must, I reflected, not without a slight trace of cynicism and sadness as I fell asleep. They were all that was left.

Chapter Thirteen

 ONE THING I ALWAYS found interesting about Alex was that she always blamed what was wrong with the world on Texas. Although she lived there for most of her growing up years, she fervently denied she was from Texas, insisting instead she was from Colorado, where she had been born and had lived for one year. Her parents were both originally from Colorado, which furthered her insistence that she was a generations-old, native Coloradan. To her, Texas, more specifically Houston, where she lived for fifteen years (and still spent every college vacation), signified all that was flat, humid, and swelteringly hot; it was rushing from an air-conditioned house to an air-conditioned car to an air-conditioned office, and then, in the evening, back again in the reverse order. Colorado, in comparison, was all that was natural and good—mountains, green grass, cool air, healthy food. If anything was wrong with Colorado (and to say such a thing was near blasphemy) the reason of course was because Texas, or Texans, were moving in and taking over. Nothing made Alex madder than seeing Texas license plate after license plate on the cars on the road. "See," she would claim vehemently, "they are turning Colorado into little Texas; it's a conspiracy."

Most of the Texans we met during our sojourn, however, were quite nice, and even Alex had to agree, though her blind loyalty to Colorado remained. Now that she was her own working woman, she vowed she would never leave the state, and when and if she married, she would make sure that her husband felt the same way. Her last conviction hasn't quite held true, for today Alex is married and lives in Wyoming, but I can say with near certainty that if pressed for an answer, Alex will still claim herself a Coloradan.

Almost from the start, Alex and I got along remarkably well, becoming fast friends. It was impossible not to like Alex. She exuded vivacity, liked to live life with a light and lively touch, enjoying parties, adventure, and boys (I say this in plural for she was pretty, outgoing, and popular and at this time in her life never settled on one boy for too long). Alex was an active participant in all that she did, whether backpacking or cross-country skiing or river rafting, and she liked to do these things with a gathering of people around her for camaraderie. I was more introspective, a person who loved life but tended to worry too much over things, and maybe it was these contrasting traits that at first made people single me out as the culprit for all that was wrong with the Chimney Rock falcons, while blithe Alex, at least at first, seemed to escape blame.

Alex's social nature never tired of trying to draw me out among her friends. She loved to talk about all the acquaintances she had made at the Forest Service, especially the young foresters and engineers, and long before I met them, I knew of Justin—tall, bearded, stern-faced mountain man type; and Clint, thin and pale and an intellectual (rather a bore, in her opinion); Mike, fun but drank too much and a bit too wild; and John, the catch of them all—a young, tall, dark, very handsome French Canadian engineer who was new this year, so still a bit mysterious. The girls were uninteresting, she said, less adventuresome and even dull, except for "Feather," a nickname for Nancy, who was outspokenly opinionated and a radical feminist.

Probably if I hadn't been discouraged from our recent setback and in need of a change of scenery, I wouldn't have let Alex talk me into accompanying her to the Fourth of July dance in Los Piños, which, as she explained enthusiastically, was the biggest event of the year for the region. Alex had been there twice. The dance was held in the old grange hall just out of town and the country western "stars" (actually local boys from Mancos, Colorado) drew everyone from all around— farmers, ranchers, merchants, Forest Service employees—any poor soul who might be drifting by. Alex was dying to go and pleaded with me to go with her while in the same breath smoothly promising we would work a full day at Chimney Rock and stay only for a few evening hours.

Against my better judgment, I went, but I began regretting my decision almost at once, for I sat white-knuckled in the truck while Alex, in her excitement, skillfully tore down the mountain road and then down the highway at forty miles an hour, a breakneck speed for a garbage truck, never minding that the top heavy vehicle swayed threateningly side to side with each near-missed pothole or curve in the road. By the time we reached the grange hall, I was already a dither of jangled nerves, and the blaring music which vibrated beneath my feet made the matter of stability essential as I groped for the nearest wall. After the weeks of calming stillness on the mountain, the shrill sounds emanating from the amplified electric guitars seemed a virulent attack on my ears. Alex, however, didn't mind in the slightest. Always generous to a fault, she insisted on paying for both of us, and I could see that she was in her element, feet tapping, bright eyes scanning the hall for her friends, whom she greeted with enthusiatic hugs when she found them.

But the sight of so many people packed into one room was surprisingly refreshing, like stepping back into the human race after spending a month in a space ship. Most of the faces were unfamiliar, but I spotted some people I knew: Edna, the cafe owner; the blonde secretary from the Forest Service, swinging a glass of beer from her hand and blithely talking to the foresters who had been so rude to me my first day on the job; Mr. Fitch, dressed in his brown Forest Service pants and a snappy cowboy shirt with an eye-catching bolo tie. I found it hard to believe he could be so daring.

Alex tugged at my sleeve to introduce me to her friends from past years as they congregated around her, regarding her like some long-lost survivor from a wilderness expedition. She was understandably reveling in the attention. From her apt descriptions, I could pick out which people were which even before introduced. Clint was hanging back, longing to be part of the action but too shy. Feather was just now in argumentative posture with some man, calling him for all to hear a sexist pig. Mike had obviously had too much to drink, even at this early hour. And there was another fellow, ruggedly good-looking with fine eyes, that I suspected must be the new young engineer. Our eyes met through the crowd, he smiled, and I could feel my face blush. This was utterly ridiculous; I chided myself that at twenty-one years of age I still fell prey to that inane habit, but Alex was paying no attention to my sudden awkwardness and was thrusting a beer into my hand while pushing me toward Justin as she was being pulled to the dance floor by Mike.

Justin didn't look pleased. Behind the thick beard that camouflaged his face and neck, his eyes darted from side to side, as if he were scouting for a means of escape. After two minutes of rather forced conversation (his reticence made him as easy to talk to as one of the falcons), Alex's friend Feather rescued the situation by telling him he was going to dance with her. A troubled look crossed his face, and after consenting rather gruffly, he fled to grab another beer.

"We women have got to stick together in this business," Feather said as Justin's back retreated through the crowd. "I think it's great what you're doing, and that you don't quit even when everything's going against you. The men around here are such assholes; they'll soon learn we're here to stay. Thanks to women like you."

I didn't exactly see my job this way, and I certainly didn't feel like a martyr. The whole sex-discrimination thing hardly touched me at all, in fact, even though I was in a male-dominated field. Maybe I escaped the problems by steadfastly believing that good work and determination were what brought rewards, not whether you were a man or a woman. For as long as I could remember, I had wanted to be an ecologist, and after years of schooling, the fact that now I was really on my way was enough thrill and incentive to see me through most anything. Next would be graduate school and more research, the communication and transference of new ideas and theories, attempting to explore the unexplored. In my opinion, there was no better, no richer field to be in; the study of life itself was an endless adventure. And setbacks? Well, they had to be endured, but who of any merit had never suffered setbacks?

Alex was back from dancing, flushed and smiling gaily. The beer I held in my hand spilled as she put her arm around me, urging me to dance and participate. Before I knew it I was thrust on the dance floor with her swaggering ex-partner, while the band blasted unharmonious chords, flogging to death the percussion instruments. The leader of the band gyrated into a frenzy; the crowd appreciated it immensely. That the music was really terrible didn't seem to matter a bit. Even I enjoyed it, for something about the close, heaving bodies, each dancing separately but together, the laughing faces, the little children running around yelling, blended into one small-town humanity; and for a while I forgot all about the peregrines, reveling only in the touch and smell and sweat of people.

After my first dance I was not without a partner again, for women were scarce and men plentiful. And either I wasn't recognized by most of the people or they were too drunk to care, but few spoke to me of the falcons, and those that did were more inquisitive than hostile. Only one man, a hardware store employee who had glasses that kept slipping off his nose, and a heavy foot, broached the subject that the falcons were not wanted here and I should mind my own business. However, he had some interesting facts for me. Where he came up with them I never knew, but in any case he insisted that he had training as a scientist and that he knew without question that peregrine falcons were from Africa. They had been brought over by the slave traders on their ships and therefore should be shipped back to where they belonged—as soon as possible.

Only one dance I remembered vividly, from beginning to end, and that was with the dark-haired engineer who for some reason sent me into a fluster any time he approached. Up close, I could tell that he was younger than I'd first thought—close to my age, I guessed—and his clear brown eyes reflected a refined humor and intelligence that looked oddly out of place in the dance hall. He had a calm self-confidence that appeared genuine, not self-inflated, which I found intriguing, but quickly I squelched all my feelings. For I knew I'd never be seeing him again, and I did not wish to be counted among the other girls I could see hovering about him on the sidelines. His name was odd and hard to pronounce—Houle, John Houle. It was French; his ancestors came from Quebec, though he was from Connecticut. Laughingly, he said it was a hell of a name for people to remember. I could have told him that his face and his whole demeanor were not difficult to remember, especially when I found myself thinking about him many times when alone on Chimney Rock, but I never would have breathed that to anyone. Once back on the mountain, Alex's guitar playing turned to country-western love songs for several weeks, and at night she would pause and wonder what all her friends were doing in town.

But all the time I knew her, Alex never complained. In fact, she thrived on the primitive, isolated conditions we shared, and as she did with everything of importance to her, she gave her whole heart to the peregrines. She took pride in accepting the blame, or credit, for the uproar that was provoked by the Chimney Rock birds. As a Coloradan, she believed she held the one true wildlife ethic, and when I questioned her about the Coloradans who wished the wildlife would vanish, thus freeing the way for economic development, she had a firm reply.

"Don't be silly. Those people aren't Coloradans. The people of my state love their wildlife. It's those from Texas—the ones who are moving here in droves—they're the ones you have to watch. The problem isn't Colorado, Marcy," she said in her sweet, high-pitched, Texas drawl. "It's Texas."

Chapter Fourteen

EARLY IN THE SECOND week of July, Alex and I caught a glimpse of the two young peregrines, well feathered now but with patches of down still sprouting comically from their bodies, peeking out from the eyrie. From the first moment, it was obvious the two were an inseparable pair; wherever one trudged along, the other crawled immediately behind. From their smaller size, I ascertained they were two males, and nearing six weeks old, they were on the verge of fledging at any minute, though they still seemed terrible cowards, beating their wings and screaming as they jumped up and down, never daring to take off and fly. I couldn't say I blamed them, with a 360-foot drop-off looming below me, I probably would have never left the nest.

Arthur once again was heralding his return home from a hunt, apparently for the benefit of the nestlings. Hearing his call, they both got mad with excitement, flapping their wings so fast they often were lifted off the ground a foot or more. One nestling, each time he found himself aloft, squealed a high-pitched "Ki-Ki-Ki!" In fact, I noticed this bird drew attention to himself whenever he moved at all; even when waddling from one small ledge to another on the cliff top, he shouted for all of heaven to hear. He was the less adept of the two: trying to run, he would fall down; trying to climb, he would more often than not slide down backwards on his rear; and trying to follow his brother into some of the more difficult nooks and crannies on the ridge top, he would trip and land on his beak. His sibling rarely did such things. But the bird seemed little distressed by his lack of agility; what he lacked in finesse, he made up for in sheer lung power.

Arthur, at first, was not selective as to whom he would give the prey procured from his sorties. He left it up to them to fight it out, getting out of the foray as soon as possible, and the selfish nature of the little birds was apparent at once as they dashed to the food and tried to snatch it away from each other. When young peregrines fledge, they continue to eat significantly more than adults, to build up their stores of fat. What this meant in graphic terms was that the birds reveled in competition over food. Usually the more physically advanced, bold and aggressive nestling was the first to get it.

July 12 was a typical day in the life of nearly fledged peregrines. Arthur dropped off what looked to be a redwing blackbird, and the more aggressive falcon lunged for the food, dragging it away as fast as he could along the ridge top. It was a decidedly difficult task, for the prey was almost as big as he and in his haste, the young falcon continually tripped over the hunk of food hanging from his beak. The sibling who always seemed to come second in everything followed in slow pursuit, and because his brother was loaded down and he unfettered, he soon caught up with the fleeting bird and lunged for the piece of food.

What ensued was a tug of war. The selfish sibling used every tactic he could to keep the food all for himself—screaming, clawing, nipping—but the treasure split in half anyway. In his frenzy the falcon decided to take what was left, and scurried off.

The timid sibling was most pleased with the situation. Quickly, he grabbed up the spoils. Puffed-up with pride, he dragged it along the rock, climbing steadily higher until he had reached the very top of the cliff. With a cursory survey of all the country at his command, he commenced to eat far away from his nest-mate.

Although the two young falcons often fought over food, in almost everything else they seemed to get along quite well, and they would spend hours just sitting together side by side, staring out at the new land before them. One of the birds (the less assertive one) was the more affectionate, and he would often nuzzle his brother's neck and probe for little bugs. Sometimes he even reached over to "kiss" his sibling, but this usually resulted in a beak wrestling match, with one bird straining to hold his body upright while the other tried to push him over.

The personalities of the two falcons became more recognizable each day, and Alex and I decided to name them. "Bold Leopold" was unmistakably the more courageous of the pair. "Albert" was his shadow. Because of their differences, we were not surprised that it was Bold Leopold who was the first to fledge, with Albert looking on in sheer stupefaction.

On the morning of July 14, Alex and I glanced up from our notes to check on a terrible shrieking and saw Leopold flying, terrified, low and alone, out across the cliff face. Desperate to land anywhere, he crashed upon an out-jutting rock which was angled at a slope of 45 degrees. Leopold tried to grasp the rock with all his might, but could not remain stable on such a precarious perch. Backward he slid down the boulder. He flapped, he screeched, but in his misery he saw that no one was coming to rescue him; and now, in desperate straits, he took off again and attempted to fly back to the eyrie.

It didn't work. Leopold was too low and too lacking in energy, and with the cliff looming high above him, the situation seemed hopeless. He landed again, yet luckily this time on a level perch, and once positioned, proceeded to screech for help. Three hours later he was still caterwauling.

Albert sat unmoving at the cliff top, watching, but growing bored. At last, Leopold decided the only one that could help him was himself. He placed one foot in front of the other and started to *climb* the rock, and thus began making slow but definite headway. Progress, however, was abruptly brought to a halt when the young falcon was confronted with a sheer face of the cliff. With a clamor he leaped into the air. Wings flapping like two electric beaters set on the whip cycle, he propelled himself with intense effort back to the eyrie. This was his first real flight—about fifteen seconds!

After this horrifying exhibition, Albert rushed back to the eyrie and refused to leave the security of the nest for the rest of the day.

Two days later, Leopold tested his rapidly growing prowess by taking three quick jaunts around the rock. At well-placed intervals he paused to perch and rest. His flights had grown to a minute, and he flaunted his pride over these dashing excursions. Albert's beak was out of joint. He wanted nothing to do with such things, for he still preferred to walk to his point of destination, vocally expressing in loud wails his dislike for ever having to fly. His brother's activities were distasteful, and he wished to ignore them, and him, period. But as Leopold continued to progress, Albert could not help watching, and in actuality he was storing up all of these things in his mind, just waiting for the right time, the right place, to make his own big splash.

But before he could muster the courage, Bold Leopold

advanced beyond him again. Taking Alex and me quite by surprise, Leopold, on his third postfledging day, attempted a small stoop. Pulling his wings back and closing up in true falcon form, he suddenly swooped down, cutting through the wind, and raced by the cliff. It was a clumsy effort, but a first.

Unfortunately, upon attempting to land after this show of sheer courage and ability, Leopold forgot to apply his brakes and crashed upon the rock ledge, somersaulting over onto his beak. This little bit of indignity did not phase him, however.

At two o'clock the same day, we observed another example of Leopold's rapid maturation. Arthur, returning from another of his innumerable hunts, carried a large bird and wailed as he approached within thirty to forty feet of the eyrie. Instantly he was greeted in midair by his intrepid fledgling, and before we knew it, there was a food exchange! Arthur came up from below, flipped upside down and raised his talons with prey for Bold Leopold to grasp. Leopold reached out his talons and clenched it. Now, flying with the dangling, precious food— made all the more so by his successful and very grown-up endeavor—Leopold soared just below the top of the cliff, perched, and ate his well-deserved meal with pride.

Albert, in contrast, had not come out from the eyrie since noon.

At 3:25, Arthur arrived back again from a hunt, this time with food expressly for Albert. Swooping near the eyrie and wailing, Arthur tried enticing his less adventurous fledgling to fly out to him as Leopold had done.

Albert did not move.

Again, Arthur tried to inveigle Albert to attempt an aerial food exchange by dangling the food right in front of the hungry nestling's beak.

Albert responded only by screeching louder.

Arthur gave up. He turned to fly directly into the eyrie but, at the very moment he did so, out barreled Albert. The two birds just barely escaped a head-on collision. Poor Albert was undone. Flapping frantically, but flying, Albert zoomed past his parent, not stopping until fifteen feet from the eyrie. Arthur slowly flew to him and deposited the catch at his feet.

Meticulously, Albert picked up and held his prey in one talon. He cocked his head. Waddling to a small crevice in the rock, he squeezed, with difficulty, into the nook. For the next half hour he feasted like a king, poking his head out now and then from the little cave to spit plucked feathers with a pucker on his face.

He had made his splash.

Chapter Fifteen

FLEDGLING PEREGRINE falcons require at least six weeks of continual hunting and flying practice before they are able to live independently. In my opinion, however, six weeks seemed a short childhood in which to learn so much; it would rush by before they ever had the slightest idea what was happening to them. Yet, after that time, Albert and Leopold would be, in scientific terms, "adults," even though in many respects they would still show signs of immaturity and youth. Their body and feather growth would be nearly completed, but their plumage would still be "immature." They wore cloaks of a different color—the crowns of their heads were a cinnamon brown, lightly streaked with black, in contrast to Arthur's jet-black helmet. The upper part of their bodies was also brown, not the bluish-gray of an adult, and their breasts and bellies were a sand color, broadly streaked with chestnut lines, quite unlike Arthur's breast of snow white that revealed only a faint streaking left over from youth. For a year or more, the fledglings would wear this dress, until they molted into adult plumage. But they would always be stuck with their big, yellow feet, which right now looked disproportionately large and cumbersome, probably because they hadn't quite learned how to use their appendages and still spent many anguished moments tripping along the ledge of the cliff.

Especially Albert. Things always came a little harder for Albert. Even his first long solo flight left something to be desired. He had grown tired watching Leopold's boring little performances of circling repeatedly around Chimney Rock, knowing, of course, that he could do just as well if he so desired; and at last he decided to prove this to his sibling. Lurching off the ledge where he sat, Albert began his first circumnavigation of the Rock, while Alex and I looked on with interest. For a few feet, Albert flew quite well, flapping his wings at a hysterical clip, but before long he began losing altitude.

Down, down, down the fledgling fell, with the slow grace of a parachutist. He continued circling around the Rock as he descended, and just before he landed on the ground, he had made the complete trip.

Totally out of character, Albert for once did not scream, but instead quietly seemed to ponder the situation. He shook his feathers, being careful to remove little pieces of twigs that stuck to his belly, and laid his wings neatly on his back. Then he leaned over to pick his toes. These necessities attended to, he started exploring. He shuffled unhurriedly around the base of the Rock, wandering in and out of boulders and pausing occasionally to confront a bush. Albert resembled more an absent-minded professor cogitating on a monumental theory than a bird who had just fallen from the nest. Obviously he felt in no danger or hurry to return home. Bold Leopold squawked from the eyrie, but Albert ignored him. Seeing a mound of dirt, he kicked at it with his feet then tried tasting it. He spat it out. Then he ate a leaf of a serviceberry bush. Now serviceberry plants are a staple to a host of animals, ranging from elk and deer to rabbits, rodents, and black bears. Indians historically dried and pressed the berries into cakes and made pemmican, a diet that lasted them throughout the year. But the berries are never consumed by birds of prey. Albert seemed to enjoy the flavor and ate another. To him, the ground must have had its advantages. A bird didn't have to worry about getting hurt by falling to the ground—he was already there. And there were plenty of things to eat, even if they tasted a bit strange. And things stayed put—no need to waste time chasing after dinner if he was hungry. As an added bonus, the feel of earth was infinitely softer than a rock ledge. No one had told Albert yet that any respectable peregrine falcon was a creature of the air, and that only land birds browse on the ground. Too, there were many unpleasant side effects to living on the ground, including the major one that a bird could easily end up as someone's supper. Fortunately for Albert, he grew tired of his surroundings before a coyote or a fox found him. With frequent spurts of frenzied motion that left both Alex and me exhausted by the end, Albert somehow managed to make it back to the eyrie unharmed.

The next few days of flight practice were anything but relaxing, but after the first week was over, both fledglings had improved their skills significantly. In particular, one new game they devised proved their rapid maturation.

The contest began at the expense of Albert, at a time when he was painstakingly trying to gather the courage for his first stoop. For over an hour he had his head crooked over the cliff, his body set, his wings in position. But he wouldn't move. Suddenly exploding in a fury of motion, he dove off head first and plummeted down like a pro, taking everyone by surprise, especially, I think, himself.

Unfortunately, at this very moment, Leopold saw his chance to seize a bit of deviltry, and plunged after his brother. Because he was a better flyer, he swiftly caught up and delivered a fiery attack on poor Albert from above. Albert was understandably shaken. The fledgling wobbled from side to side, forcefully trying to regain stability, making a turn midflight to keep from crashing to the ground. Luckily, as he did so, he must have caught an air current, for he was taken speedily aloft, rising far above his brother with little expended effort. This little twist of fate bolstered his confidence, for instead of timidly rushing to the eyrie, as he was prone to do, Albert instead stretched out his legs like two wooden toothpicks and descended upon Leopold, giving him a swift, sharp poke as he passed.

Leopold was knocked off course; dramatically, he swooned downward. But quickly he regained his bearings and, seizing another air current, zoomed above Albert to retaliate. For five minutes, the fledglings rode the invisible elevators of the sky, diving at one another, and the game was deemed an immediate success, to be played countless times during the day. Albert, being inherently more lazy and less daring, I think still preferred the games they played on firm ground—tag, tug-of-war, and head-jousting (his all time favorite)—but he was always up for a rollick, especially when Leopold would fly up behind him and knock him from his perch, which he did often, a trait Leopold must have inherited from his mother and which Alex and I came to term "the gentle nudge."

Bold Leopold, in fact, was progressing so rapidly that on his tenth day post-fledging, he took a lengthy sortie all alone, whether by accident or design, after catching a monumental updraft which lifted him far above our heads. Alex and I fully expected him to come at once screeching home, but he fooled us. Alone and intrepid once again, he set out for the southwest and disappeared. He returned after being gone thirty-nine minutes—a remarkably long period spent away from the cliff.

I knew well, however, this was only the beginning. Each fledgling, in his own way, was starting to pull away from the security of his babyhood and reaching out for independence and freedom. The following day, even Albert tried leaving the home territory for an exploratory flight. He did not go far—only across to our observation ledge—and after a quick rest and a good look at us, he flew down below us, heading straight in the direction of a nesting kestrel.

This was his downfall. The unwary, innocent bird didn't realize he was crossing a forbidden line to invade another raptor's nesting territory. And almost immediately, the mother kestrel—half the size of Albert—declared war and without mercy assailed the young peregrine.

Terror stricken, Albert tore back to the cliff screaming and for the next hour refused to fly under any circumstances. As usual, he had learned his lesson the hard way. But one thing about Albert, he was never set back for long. The following day, the same little kestrel came out to attack Albert when he again passed through the invisible territorial line. This time, however, the adult tiercel was in the vicinity and stooped on the kestrel, sending it scurrying back to the nest.

Feeling secure, Albert sailed on regally. He took a short detour around the kestrel nest then perched on a ledge not ten yards from Alex and me.

Arthur, however, would not stand for this. His fledgling had not developed his fear of man and must learn. From above, Arthur pounced on Albert with an attack so fierce that Albert shrieked and bolted for the eyrie. This time he didn't peek from the nest until well after supper time. And much to my secret disappointment, never again was he to come within a quarter mile of us. Once Albert learned his lesson twice, it seemed, it didn't have to be repeated again.

Chapter Sixteen

 FORTUNATELY, THE FIRST accident of the summer was relatively minor. Alex, in her haste to pack up the gear one evening, inadvertently dropped the ten pound anamometer from the top of the lookout onto my head. The only injuries I sustained were a welt the size of a tablespoon on my forehead, which refused to fade for two weeks and turned a spectrum of colors, from rose to brown to black, and a jostled-loose gold inlay.

The loss of a filling is usually only a minor hindrance, requiring a simple visit to the dentist, but when you are deep in the wilds and the nearest village is forty miles away, all your normal options shrivel, leaving you at the mercy of fate. There was only one dentist nearby, and something about him, though no one could tell me what it was, was peculiar. Alex revealed she had never known anyone who had gone to him; all her acquaintances opted instead to drive over a hundred additional miles to Durango for their dental work. I didn't have time for that and, anyway, I reasoned, regluing a gold filling should be a snap for anyone.

That faith was my mistake.

The following day, I left Alex alone on the mountain and drove to town for the first time in weeks. Nearing the dentist's office, I began noticing signs advertising his services. Having been raised in a doctor's family, I learned at an early age that medical professionals did not advertise, as it was considered unprofessional, but giving the dentist the benefit of the doubt, I reasoned that he worried that people might miss the turnoff to his office. How they could was beyond me, however, for at the junction of his driveway he had erected a full-sized billboard adorned with dots, pointing arrows, and even a photograph of the smiling dentist himself. Below his round, bald head, in hand-painted block letters, were the reassuring words: "DON'T TURN BACK, TURN HERE!"

I should have heeded the warning and turned back instantly, but I continued innocently on, ricocheting across a washboard driveway leading to a small, brown trailer. One car, a slightly dented Ford Mustang, was parked in front. Aesthetically, the place lacked everything, but I soon discovered that the dentist more than made up for its uninviting appearance by his personal attentiveness. Before I had cut the engine, he appeared on the steps to escort me inside, smiling the same felicitous grin as on the billboard.

"You are in luck," he said graciously. "Believe it or not, I have no other appointments at the moment. Please, won't you come in."

Something about the way he gripped my arm made me suspect he had not had any appointments all day, perhaps even longer. I was skillfully guided to the dentist's chair with time only for a swift glance at the outmoded office.

"No receptionist?"

"I don't believe in them. Saves on overhead."

Stubby fingers (definitely not the hands of a surgeon) arranged a fraying plastic apron around my neck. "Don't you have a dental assistant?" I asked.

"Why have an assistant when I can do everything better

myself? And just what happened to you," he asked, patting my bruised forehead.

"Oh, I had a little accident on Chimney Rock; nothing serious."

"Chimney Rock!" He stepped back and squinted to see me more clearly. "So you must be the Bird Girl, the little celebrity! It's my lucky day."

I didn't care to ask what he meant. The room seemed very hot, and something about its decor made me uneasy. I couldn't decide what it was. The equipment appeared clean and polished, the floor was scrubbed—it even smelled of detergent—and the curtains and chairs were definitely faded but not tattered.

Humming to himself, the dentist fondled his instruments, leaving the impression he wasn't clear which to use. Taking a deep breath, he poised himself over my mouth like a sculptor eager to dig into a block of marble.

"My only request, a little one, is that you lie still and don't talk. Think about something calming, soothing, like a black velvet curtain blowing in the breeze, or a cemetery."

Plunging fingers from both hands into my mouth, he began exploring, stretching my cheeks at impossible angles as he repeatedly positioned his mirror to see better. "Not so good," he said, frowning. "No, not so good."

I had been to a dentist before I came to Chimney Rock, and I knew my teeth were sound, so his judgment was suspect. Driving deeper inside my mouth, he spread my sun-chapped lips to their limits, and I winced as they cracked.

"What did I say? Don't move. Lie back." Gently he laid his hand on my shoulder and pushed me back in the chair. "Dammit," he growled, fumbling about the tray with one hand. "Where is that inlay, that little sucker?"

"T-T-Table—"

"What? Oh, on the table! Good girl! All right, you dirty little thing, gotcha. Now, in you go."

He crowded the filling into my mouth, twisting and turning it around and around, then pushing it down with palpable force. "Go in, I said! Oh, for crying out loud," he exclaimed, taking it out again and freeing my mouth of his wretched hands. "This is just a gold piece of junk. It doesn't fit! Young lady, your teeth must have shifted."

"Shifted!"

"Yes. The only thing I can do, short of scrapping this all together, is file down that tooth in front of the bad one. Yes, that's the answer. I'll get my jack-hammer here—just kidding. It's a drill. Just sounds like it belongs with a construction crew. Won't hurt a bit."

Both hands again shoved my head against the headrest.

"Teef shiff ovo-nite?" I choked.

"What? Yes, yes, overnight. Happens that way sometimes. I hate to tell you, but all your fillings are bad. What you need are crowns. Crowns are the wave of the future; they're far superior. Cost a bit more, but hell, what's the price of a beautiful smile? Not that yours isn't nice. Your teeth are white and straight. Braces, eh? But they won't look that way for long if they all fall out."

He tried the inlay again. "Son of a . . . still doesn't go in right. Know what I think? I think that front tooth must not have been the problem after all. Gee, I'm sorry about that!"

"Doctor, really—"

"But I see the culprit! I don't need to tell you you wouldn't have these problems if you had crowns. The tooth above the inlay has shifted, the shifty old cuss. I'll file down that nasty cusp—don't need it anyway—and the filling will go in smooth as cream. Please don't talk! I can't work if you're twitching your lips."

I cringed at the sight of the drill coming out again.

"Don't you get a little nervous being up there all by your-self?" he asked. "Or is there another one of you? Talk of iso-lation! I wouldn't like that at all. I'm a People Person. That's with capital P's. And what happens if the Indians really do go on the warpath like they are threatening? You look surprised. Don't you read the papers? The Indians, Dennis Banks and the American Indian Movement, all that stuff they're planning? I'm not an Indian, but I sympathize with them, though not to the extremes that they're taking it. This explosives thing, now; I don't believe that's the way they'll get their point across."

"Explosif—"

"Then that talk about the Utes taking back Chimney Rock. For God's sake, it's their ancestral home, never should have gone to the Forest Service in the first place. But to resort to violence, like they did in Ignacio last week . . . Aha! Cusp 'bye bye,' as my granddaughter would say. She's two. Now what's the matter? That inlay should fit. Stupid thing . . . I'm going to make it fit!"

His face swelled alarmingly as he tried to thrust the filling in place. My head pounded at the force. "Where's my ham-mer," he cried. "This thing's bent! It needs a good whack!"

"Docto—"

"What?" He released my mouth.

"Please, Doctor, may I have some water?"

"Why?"

"To . . . to wash out my mouth."

"Oh, yes, water!" he said apologetically. "Coming right up. Here you are. You can spit it out over there."

"Now, this should do it," he said striking my filling. "If it doesn't, I'll just take my hammer to your teeth! Let's give it a try. Yes, almost there now. A tad more filing down and we'll have it licked."

"Are you sure you need to file down my teeth? So many of them?"

"Does a surgeon use a scalpel? Lie back please. As I was saying, if I were you I'd watch out for those Indians. Never know when they'll paint their faces and drag you from the mountain, or worse, make you a sacrifice. Voila! What'd I tell you? All I need now is my glue. I'm warning you though—no telling how long that inlay will stay there. On the other hand, if you'd come back and let me put in a crown—"

"This will be fine, thank you."

"Your mistake. Can't say I didn't warn you! Good job, if I do say so myself. But I didn't need to file down that one tooth. Shouldn't have done that. It was a good one, and now it's left a little gap. Too bad—"

"What do you mean, gap?"

"Everything will be all right after the other teeth shift into place. If that inlay falls out again within the year, I'll put it back free of charge. I call it my service warranty. You won't find another dentist with such a guarantee."

I was sure I would not.

"There. You're smilin' pretty, little lady. What you got in your pants?"

"What?"

"I said, what do you have in your pockets. How much dinero?"

"You mean money?" I pulled out five dollars and my checkbook.

"Five dollars it is. Especially seeing I bungled that one tooth. Really, I am sorry."

"Do you have a mirror, so I could see my teeth?"

"There's the phone ringing." With a soft nudge at my back he eased me to the door. "Don't worry about that gap. It'll close after a bit. You have my word. Or if it doesn't, there's always the service warranty."

"Yes, the warranty—"

"But there's one thing even better than a warranty. That's a crown. Next time you come in, we'll see to it that all your fillings are made crowns. But you may not be able to if those Indians really do take over Chimney Rock. Then again, maybe you can reason with them."

He sighed with a wistful smile. "Just think of all those Ute Indians who need crowns."

Chimney Rock at sunset.

Chimney Rock and Companion Rock as seen from Piedra River Valley.

Chimney Rock and Companion Rock (Companion Rock in foreground) viewed from the observation post.

Marcy setting up spotting scope at the observation post, on the edge of the high mesa (old fire lookout in background).

Arthur flying over Chimney Rock.

The view from Chimney Rock.

Arthur perching on Companion Rock.

Round ceremonial room, part of Chimney Rock's "Great House"—the largest, highest, and best-built structure in the Archeological Area. It is a fine example of ancient Chacoan architecture, constructed approximately A.D. 1093.

Another view of the thirty-five-room Great House—a natural observatory of sacred significance to the Ancestral Puebloans.

Marcy leaving the observation post, next to the Great House, just before a thunderstorm hits.

Alex observing Chimney Rock peregrines from the cliff's edge.

Chimney Rock and Companion Rock as seen from below.

John at Chimney Rock observation post, at sunset.

Marcy in her new U.S. Forest Service vehicle, after the garbage truck died.

Marcy scanning cliffs in search of peregrine falcons.

Barry Layne climbing Companion Rock to the peregrine eyrie.

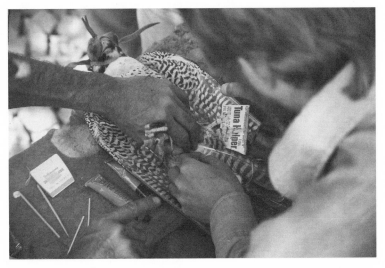

Dr. James Enderson and Don Miller sewing a telemetry monitor on Lady, the female falcon who replaced Jenny at Chimney Rock the following year.

Lady outfitted with telemetry, just before being released back into the wild.

Marcy holding a Chimney Rock peregrine.

Chapter Seventeen

 THERE WAS A GAP in my teeth, and the dentist had not been joking entirely about the Indians. On my way home from the dentist, I swung by to pick up a paper and found a short column addressing the Ute Indian skirmish in Ignacio, Colorado, that had happened a week before. Police thought it was related to the American Indian Movement's crusade to return to Indians what was once their land. State patrolmen had recently confiscated arms and explosives from militant supporters, both Indian and white, and there was growing concern over the possibility of violence erupting in the area. Nothing was mentioned about Chimney Rock, but the mountain had a highly visible profile and religious significance to the Indians.

I did not care to dwell upon it. Anyway, the falcons were so absorbing, I had little time to spare thinking about anything else. Presently, Arthur had taken on a new, important role—that of flight instructor. The fledglings had now taken to the air for two weeks, and the time had come for refining advanced techniques.

On July 25, Arthur encouraged his offspring to join him in acrobatic flying. Albert waddled to the other side of the cliff; Leopold flew to his father. For the next fifteen minutes, an amazing spectacle of parental assistance and guidance was conducted. There is some debate in scientific circles whether animals—in this case, birds—actually "teach" their offspring how to hunt. Some theorists believe it is a matter of instinct alone, parent or no parent. And young falcons have learned to fly and hunt without parental help. But I believe the process must be speeded up when fledglings are instructed by their parents in the finer matters of survival. For ten full days, Arthur devoted his time to teaching his youngsters the maneuvers they would need to become proficient hunters. By the end of that time, they resembled old veterans.

But on this first day, while Albert hid, Leopold awkwardly followed behind Arthur's lead. Arthur glided, breaking up his rhythm with quick wingbeats, as Leopold tried to copy his movements. Together, teacher and student circled, soared, and even attempted elementary stoops. At one point Arthur turned to attack Leopold; the fledgling shrieked and evaded him. The comparison between the fledgling's passionate but inept attempts to imitate and the graceful aerial ballet of Arthur's flight was comical.

When Arthur was away from the cliff, the fledglings transferred what they learned from their father to their own private games. Their favorite recreation soon became pretending they were exchanging food in midair. This amusement helped them immensely in their ability to retrieve the prey that Arthur brought home to them. The game was simple yet required great dexterity. Grasping each other by the talons while in flight, they swirled down towards the ground locked together, at the last moment releasing to rev themselves up to play it over again, up and down, up and down, squawking wildly in pure excitement like children riding on a roller coaster.

Albert and Leopold's fun didn't stop in the air, however; on firm ground, they continued playing tag, beak wrestling, and a new invention, leap frog. Albert landed on a low bush. Leopold skimmed over, just missing his head, and perched in the next bush. Albert took off again and flew over Leopold's head to land in the next bush. In this manner, they made their way all about the base of the cliff.

Albert usually won these tournaments. While Leopold was more at home in the air, Albert could outdistance him on the ground, where I think he preferred to be. Albert had even originated a pet game of his own, one that was undeniably strange, but much loved. He searched for little rocks the size of eggs and "roosted" on them, fluffing out his wings and tail feathers to sit on them just like a brooding female. Leopold did not have these maternal instincts and would leave Albert alone when he exhibited these tendencies.

By the month's end, a new milestone occurred in the fledglings' lives. For the first time, I observed their innate desire to chase and to hunt other birds. Flying for fun would still take priority for a few weeks longer, but soon the intense drive to procure prey, an instinct upon which their very survival would depend, began to gain in importance and supersede everything else in their lives.

Arthur helped it along when, on a flying expedition with both young falcons trailing behind him, he stooped on a small bird. Albert and Leopold followed, not knowing what to make of the new frolic but enjoying it considerably. With the sun behind him, Arthur did not strike the prey but, nearing it, flipped upside down, contorting to spiral up into a vortex. Wailing madly, the fledglings pumped their wings in clumsy imitation. A second time Arthur dived after a bird, this time a violet-green swallow; he missed intentionally as Leopold and Albert looked on from above.

Arthur's intended miss, for the benefit of his offspring, brought up a problem biologists encounter when attempting to determine the success ratio of peregrine hunting efforts. Some scientists believe peregrines have a distinct tendency to chase prey without desiring to kill it, in order to keep up their hunting skills, keep their eyes keen, or perhaps just to exhibit a zest for living. Other raptor scientists, however, feel these pseudo attacks are not playful at all but are true misses. Whatever the case, the data become muddied, but right now, I felt confident that Arthur had indeed no desire to make a kill, as for a third time he encouraged his young to practice the stoop. Still screaming, Albert and Leopold tried feebly. With all the fracas and commotion they produced, most of the birds of the area had already safely found cover, and the lesson was ended.

Leopold loved to practice and eagerly awaited a chance to try this new skill on his own. He had his moment two days hence when an unwary "LGB" (biologists' name for little gray bird) flew beneath him in clear shot. Leaping from the cliff, Leopold pursued the petrified little bird, who was also swooping downward in an attempt to avoid the threat of Leopold's talons. Within three feet of his prey, wings bent fiercely back and still gathering speed, Leopold unfortunately began losing control. The little bird then merely twittered to one side and left the poor fledgling to continue in his headlong dive to the earth. Upon recovering himself, Leopold found his dinner had disappeared completely and, thus subdued, flew back to the cliff to wait for Arthur.

After the fledglings realized what fun it was terrorizing all the birds in their domain, both youngsters pursued everything that moved. Ravens, turkey vultures, red tails, even the young kestrel family—nothing was spared. A visiting raptor had merely to fly within a half mile of the cliff and it would be barraged by two tormenting clouds of motion. I always felt a little sorry for these innocent, wandering hawks, who must have regarded the two pests as we humans do mosquitoes—not life threatening but severely annoying.

Albert and Leopold must also have been unnerving to Arthur. The tiercel still had the sole responsibility of providing for them, and the job was becoming more unpleasant all the time. No longer satisfied to wait for their parent to deposit food at their doorstep, the fledglings now competitively raced out from the cliff the moment Arthur was sighted returning from a hunting sortie, and the lucky one to reach him first received the prized food. The unlucky runner-up, however, proceeded to beg for his rightful share and, when it was not forthcoming, set in to harass his father for all he was worth. Screaming, diving with outstretched talons, and acting like a spoiled child, the youngster left hungry created such an uproar that Arthur was forced to depart.

By the first week of August, with the fledglings nine weeks old, I could see the time was approaching when they would be able to provide for themselves, for their repertoire of aerial loops, spins, twists, and dives—all techniques of the hunt—was rapidly improving. And with this new seriousness of purpose came the inevitable loosening of family bonds.

This was not unfortunate. Indeed not, it was healthy and desirable, especially considering that coming events would change all our lives on Chimney Rock and put an end to our stillness, isolation, and protection.

Neither Alex nor I could see that far ahead, and so we watched, not without regret, the first hints of separation between the two brothers who had always been so close. Slowly but steadily, Albert and Leopold began spending their time apart. They practiced hunting and flying at different times of day and at different places. The intense interest in games, especially games played together, was diminishing, and in its place was the ambition to hunt, to explore, to find independence. Alone.

Only at night did the brothers' dependence on one another flagrantly show itself. Albert would not sleep alone. Whatever he was doing prior to the time, at dusk he would drop everything to find Leopold.

Leopold didn't mind. And for a while longer, the two young peregrines sat together very, very close, waiting for the night's sky to shower them with the brightness of its stars and for Arthur to come home.

Chapter Eighteen

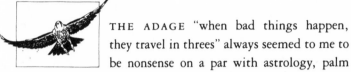

THE ADAGE "when bad things happen, they travel in threes" always seemed to me to be nonsense on a par with astrology, palm reading, and tarot cards. I was an optimist; I believed in the power of positive thinking. However, by the end of my first summer at Chimney Rock, although I remained an optimist, I had become a convert to the negative threes axiom.

The second accident of the summer was a result of our study of peregrine food habits. Now that the fledglings were gaining self-sufficiency and spending more time away from the cliff, there was little danger of the falcons abandoning the nest if man disturbed them on occasion. For the purpose of determining the prey species they were eating, Barry Layne requested that we traverse the fearsome knife-edge ridge to the base of the eyrie and search around for any prey remains the peregrines might have dropped.

I despised the task. When the falcons were home, it disturbed them; when they were away, it was still unpleasant because I had to avoid the yellow jacket nest and watch my step as I probed through the jagged boulders strewn at the base of the rock. We kept the mauled, decomposing remains, generally wings, which are left untouched in peregrine kills, in a cooler filled with dry ice. In later years biologists would collect samples of local prey species and send them on to

Patuxent Laboratory in Maryland, where scientists would chemically analyze the body tissue for levels of DDE, PCBs, chlorinated hydrocarbons, and other toxic substances.

Barry suspected, and rightly so, that the peregrines were still getting a goodly dose of deadly DDT, whose use, but not production, had for the most part been banned in the United States. The crux of the problem is that the pesticide, because it is cheap and available, continues to be heavily applied in poorer, developing countries. Migrating birds, the kinds that the native peregrines depend on for food, get loaded with the toxic chemical during winter months when residing in South American countries. They bring it back home in their tissues in the spring and summer, and the peregrines ingest the poisons in concentrated levels.

Many scientists believe that until DDT is banned worldwide and less harmful substances for controlling insects are produced inexpensively, the problems will continue and the existence of peregrines, other raptors, and migratory birds will continue to be threatened.

So, as Barry and scientists like him set out to prove this theory, they needed more conclusive information, and people working in the field such as Alex and me did much of the legwork for them. Late in the afternoon of a hot day, when I was fatigued and not watching prudently as I scrambled over the rocks on hands and feet, climbing to places I shouldn't have climbed and wouldn't have attempted if I had had my wits about me, I noticed the decaying remains of a scrub jay lying in a crack between the boulders below me. Stretching for it, I misplaced my footing and splayed headlong, arms flailing, and with ungainly accuracy missed everything that would have softened the blow, colliding chin-first with the apex of a whetted boulder eight feet below.

My hands dangled in the cranny between two rocks as my legs sprawled uphill behind me. Dazed but conscious, I took account of my body. I could move my arms and legs; therefore my neck was not broken. I detected no broken bones. Two levels of rocks below I saw my binoculars lying battered, probably ruined. Alex yelled from the lookout while Arthur screeched above.

Sluggishly pulling myself to my feet, I looked down, surprised to see the rock drenched with blood, my blood—my face! Putting a filthy paw to my chin, I sensed little feeling, but staring somewhat cross-eyed, I saw blood pouring though my fingers and a flap of something dangling.

My jaw?

Waves of nausea standard to such situations forced me to close my eyes. Soon Alex was at my side. Her face blanched and, averting her eyes, she tore off the bandana she wore over her hair, crushing it into my hands.

"Here—put pressure on your . . . your chin. Try to stop the bleeding."

"How bad is it? Alex, talk to me! What's this piece hanging?"

"It's . . . well, it was your chin. Marcy, you've got to see a doctor—"

"My chin is gone?"

"We've got to get help. Can you walk?"

"I don't feel well, Alex."

"We've got to get you out of here. Hold on to me."

Somehow I made it back across the boulders and ridge to the lookout. Alex hustled me along, and limply I followed her to the truck like an old, faithful dog. One side of me fought to look in the rear view mirror to assess the damage to my face; the other, wiser side made me refrain. Time seemed to be at a standstill, and I was not panicked, though I knew Alex was nervous, judging by her pallor and almost maniacal driving to town. It worried me that she resisted looking at me the entire drive, even when stopping at a nearby farmhouse to use the phone and alert the local medical center that we were coming.

Was it that bad? The farmer sallied outside to gawk and wordlessly backed inside, crushing my morale. "Darn it all!" Alex cried, climbing in. "That's the problem with these little towns!"

"What problem?"

"No doctors, or at least when you need them."

"No doctors! Alex!"

"Oh, I shouldn't have said that! There is a doctor—one of him—but he's out of town. Saturday, you know. But the nurse said the medical practitioner's on call, and he'll be there to meet us."

"But it's my face, Alex!"

"I know it's your face! But she said confidentially you'd be better off with the technician 'cause he's better than the doctor. Better at things like stitching wounds."

"Let's go to the hospital in Durango—"

"We don't have time. Anyway, everything'll be all right. Trust me."

The speed of Alex's driving increased in direct proportion with her anxiety. I wondered if I should ever again see my old face staring out at me from the mirror; it may not have been glamorous, but at least it had a chin!

The slim young practitioner opened the door and led us inside with casual indifference. He asked me to remove the blood-stained bandana. I tugged gently at it, and as the scarf dropped from my face, I saw to my horror that a sizable chunk of my chin did too.

The close-set eyes of the technician bugged. "My God!" he cried comfortingly. "Why didn't you say it was that bad!"

"I explained it to the nurse," exclaimed Alex.

"Sit down, sit down over here."

The technician's consoling bedside manner made me suddenly want to cry, and I know I would have broken into tears then and there if something else hadn't happened at the same instant which was so shocking that I forgot my misery at once and felt only potent embarrassment.

Out from the examining room he walked—the young engineer, the handsome young engineer I had met at the dance and had thought about all too often on long, quiet evenings with nothing to do. Those same sparkling, merry brown eyes looked into mine. Now they held only concern, concern for this hideous, disfigured creature who was covered with blood, grime, and sweat and didn't have a chin.

"Please, if you'll come in the examining room," said the practitioner. "We only have one; so you'll have to excuse the lack of privacy. Peterson, old man, can you wait a minute with that arm?"

Mr. Peterson, a Forest Service employee whose arm hung in a makeshift sling, nodded agreeably. "She looks like she needs you more than me."

Pointing for me to recline on the examining table, the practitioner began scrubbing up. "Just what did you do to yourself?"

"Fell over a cliff."

"Fell over a . . . yes, that's something we all aspire to do once in a lifetime. And what were you doing on this cliff, if I may be so bold?"

"Watching birds."

"Aaaaaaa, very interesting. Watching birds, and fell over a

cliff. Well, your chin may have saved your life. Do you realize that if you landed merely one inch higher you probably wouldn't have any teeth right now? One inch lower and you'd have severed your jugular? As it is, with the impact you've had, it's miraculous you didn't break your jaw with the impact."

"My jaw's not broken then?"

"If it were, you wouldn't be talking. Then I'd be forced to rig a nifty device so you couldn't move your jaw for a month or more, and you'd speak through a tiny opening in your lips and eat strained foods through a straw. You're a lucky girl."

"But will she have a chin?" Alex asked to the point.

"She'll have a chin, of some sort." He inspected more closely my face. "Yes, you'll have a chin. But it will take a while to reconstruct it. I'll need some help; John, will you act as my assistant?"

"Certainly."

"And you, miss," he said to Alex, "you can hold this poor thing's hand and say there-there while I try stitching up this chaos. Cover her face with this sheet, leave only the chin showing, will you John?"

John smiled warmly into my eyes, trying to act like nothing was significantly wrong with my face, though I knew better. What must he think of me, lying here on this table like an idiot? Alex was profoundly examining her feet so as not to look at my face and digging her fingernails into my flesh. I had been wishing for another meeting with John, not at a silly dance, but one where I felt on my own ground, sure of myself, in control. Anything but this. Alex gripped my hand harder as the technician shot the novocaine into what remained of my chin. He was displeased with the dozens of pieces of infinitesimal grit pummeled in the open wound.

"This is going to take a long time. You better sit down,

John. Arm going to last, Peterson?"

"Yup."

"Crimeny—what a way to spend a Saturday."

Time dragged on wooden legs as I lay under the little sheet that covered my face, body stiff on the table, surrounded by pitying people. Alex remained oddly still, but John did not, assuring me repeatedly that I was going to look terrific, that the technician was getting every last piece of needless junk out of my chin. When Alex left to go to the bathroom, he even held my hand. Being unable to see, I liked the feel of his big hand with long, sensitive fingers. I could never like a man with fat fingers. My feelings ranged from deathly humiliation to feeling sorry for myself to worrying I was going to faint from the closeness of the little room and especially from all the heat I was generating under the head sheet. My feet had gone to sleep; thousands of little needles were going off. What seemed like hours later when the practitioner at last began stitching up my face—two layers worth, one subcutaneous and one superficial—everyone sighed with exhaustion.

Somehow it was over. The sheet was removed from my face, and the practitioner began rolling out bandages.

"You're going to be so bandaged up you'll look like Santa Claus with a white beard," he said.

"Santa Claus!"

"He's pulling your leg," John put in.

"Oh, yes she will." Skillfully, he wrapped the lower half of my face with long bandages that stretched from ear to ear. "There. Hi, Santa. You have a chin."

Alex moaned with relief. "Doctor, I didn't think you could do it!" she said, giving my hand a squeeze.

John helped me to my feet. With utmost difficulty, I looked at him, for I liked him now more than ever before and did not want his pity, even if I looked like Santa Claus—I could see that much in the mirror. The practitioner shoved into my hand something to take, told me to buy some Tylenol, and asked that I see him or the doctor, preferably the doctor, in a week. His attention finally turned to the sprained elbow of the poor Forest Service officer, whom John had brought in over two and a half hours ago.

"Ugliest looking chin I ever saw," the technician casually remarked while preparing to x-ray Mr. Peterson's arm. "But someday she won't even remember this day."

"I doubt that!" he remarked.

"Only her scar will reveal the truth. And it's going to be a dandy."

When I got to the car, I cried. All this nonsense, and John too! I felt more determined than ever to see him again some-day, someday when I wasn't pathetic, hideous, and helpless.

But the peregrines couldn't tell any difference, and soon the solace of the wilderness assuaged my wounded vanity. Face injuries heal quickly, and in less than a year my chin had mended so well no one even bothered mentioning it. No one except my five-year-old nephew. Children are always more honest than adults. Looking me over carefully at Christmas that year, he was utterly mesmerized by my chin, which he thought I'd had tattooed.

"That's swell!" he cried, reaching up to feel it. "What a neat picture of a bird. Can you put one on my chin too?"

Now, ten years later, the scar fully healed and faded with time, faint traces of lines yet remain, weaving across my chin in a peculiar shape. Oddly, they resemble the pointed, upturned wings of a bird in flight—of a flying peregrine falcon.

Chapter Nineteen

OBSERVING WILD ANIMALS can be incredibly fatiguing, especially in the heat of late July and early August. With Albert and Bold Leopold nearing ten weeks old and four weeks post-fledging, the bustling activity that had entertained us all summer was dwindling. The falcons spent progressively less time at the cliff itself. Most of the animals of the area were done for the year raising families. August was the beginning of slack time; the whirlwind of spring migration and the seasonal breeding period were over. It was a time of growing maturity and of training and testing wings.

For a wildlife biologist, this was a time to begin to shift gears, to start rehashing notes and analyzing data. The "field season" was not over—not for a couple of months yet—but the flurry of excitement requiring extra long working hours was abating. Now there were even longer stretches of inactivity between exciting glimpses into the animal world, and sometimes these became (do I, as a committed naturalist, dare say it?) periods of boredom.

The stifling weather and extended periods of sitting immobile were a fatal combination. When hours dragged with little to watch, it was too easy to fall asleep at the lookout. To the best of my knowledge, Alex never committed this unpardonable sin. But I did. Several times in the ninety-five degree

August heat, Alex caught me gazing at the falcons with only one eye open. Fortunately, most days there was something absorbing to watch, like the fledgling kestrel playing loop the loop with a neighboring Clark's nutcracker or the feisty ravens experimenting with their myriad of calls and squawks as they roughhoused by the hour.

And, of course, Albert, when he was home, was always entertaining. Albert had flair when it came to doing things his "own" way, not the typical peregrine way. He was an adventurer, not in the same fashion as his brother, who flew great distances and was the first to try the new, sophisticated maneuvers, but rather as a connoisseur of the homely things. Albert explored rocks. He took pleasure in sampling bushes now and then. He was continually curious about species other than his own. And he made friends. Before the fledging kestrel was seven weeks old, Albert had formed a relationship with it, as well as with the neighboring Swainson's hawk. He flew to greet them when they passed by. One thing that seemed to confuse Albert was that if he was to eat, he would someday have to learn to make a kill. The concept was over his head; at this stage, he still preferred playing with his prey species, not hunting them.

In August, however, this changed. On the day of my twenty- second birthday, Albert took us by complete surprise by attempting his first kill. This was a hallmark, for it meant a leap in development, and it should have been noteworthy except for one small thing. Albert chose to forgo hunting his small-sized flying companions—appropriate peregrine food—and instead set his culinary sights on a bug. A big bug.

It is true that other birds of prey are bug eaters. Red tails have been known to eat grasshoppers. Kestrels largely subsist on insects and mice. And the large, graceful Swainson's hawk will sometimes live entirely on locusts. But peregrines? No. That was demeaning. Albert, however, didn't realize this, and the large bug, which through my binoculars looked to be a dragonfly, thoroughly captivated him. It flew about entrancingly, hovering from one side of Albert's beak to another, but Albert, though he earnestly tried, could not catch it. He pounced in the air after the bug and, for all his flying effort, more closely resembled a fat pigeon than a sleek falcon. I admired him for his persistence, but the job was too much for him. After this attempt, Albert gave up the pursuit of bugs. The following day he returned to practicing stoops, which, considering his survival, proved a much wiser choice.

Fortunately for Alex and me, we didn't have to depend solely on our poor hunting skills to eat. As summer progressed, our meals became substantially more plain and lackluster, largely because when the ambient temperature went up, our fresh food spoiled more quickly. Yet neither of us ever complained, though at certain times, I would have almost killed for a fresh green salad, a bowl of raspberries with cream, a ten-ounce slice of rare rib-eye steak. These perishable delicacies were unmentionables between us. Luxury for us was hot chocolate, the richer and chocolatier the better, and we would sip this with relaxed satisfaction around the campfire in the evenings while playing songs on our guitars. Alex was quite the entertainer and had a good singing voice. Some she loved playing over and over again, especially her all time favorite, "When It's Crying Time Again."

Living with Alex for two months, I found her most appealing trait was her continual thoughtfulness. She proved this most endearingly to me on my birthday, when I was forced to be away from all family and friends, parties, cards, and presents. Alex was determined I should not feel neglected or lonely on this special day and, after work, astonished me by revealing a sack of mail, with which she had absconded from the Forest Service the day of my accident, two days before, and which held birthday cards and loving wishes from all those dear to me. Alex had made a card for me too, with little drawings showing significant falcon events of the summer and with a poem about our life together on the mountain.

I noticed a card with handwriting I couldn't recognize. Opening it, I saw it was from John Houle. Nothing serious was said, only lighthearted well-wishes that my face would heal quickly and nothing else would befall me. Quickly I put it aside, pretending it was nothing, but keen-eyed Alex was utterly delighted.

"Aren't you surprised?" she cried. "He's so smart and good-looking and nice. Every girl I know is after him."

"That's what's wrong with him." But the problem was, there wasn't anything else wrong with him; from our brief encounters, he seemed honest and sincere, but with the ridiculous situation at the medical center, I had spoiled everything.

"And I have another surprise," Alex said, backing slowly into the trailer. "You'll never guess in a hundred years." She disappeared inside, and returned a few seconds later with a brown paper bag. "Well, open it!"

"Steaks!"

"Two luscious top sirloin steaks thickly cut, just the way we've been hallucinating about them."

"But Alex, where will we cook them? Certainly not fried on the Coleman. Over the campfire?"

"No. I will broil them in the stove."

"The stove? The stove doesn't work."

"Aha! That's where you're wrong. In town when you were

wandering around all doped up, I went to the Forest Service, and Mr. Fitch was there! Can you believe it? Someone there on a Saturday? So I got our mail, and Fitch stopped to chat. He brought up the wretched news that in a week he's coming up here and bringing with him a contractor to look over the place. He plans some work for this summer, in preparation for the swarms of tourists he dreams of."

I moaned.

"That's what I thought. But he's beside himself with joy. Anyway, he brought up again, like a broken record, that two girls shouldn't be alone up here and all that jazz and asked for the thousandth time about the accommodations, and I mentioned for the thousandth time we were doing just fine, even though nothing in the trailer worked. He looked shocked, as if my words finally clicked with him. My question is why they didn't click before, but he got all choked up and insisted the stove worked, that all it needed was to be hooked up a certain way to the propane tanks outside. I tried it yesterday. It worked! Can you believe it? I could have been baking things all summer!"

Alex's eyes were dreamy. She was a true domestic, whereas I was not; I'd drooled repeatedly over her stories of the cakes, pies, and cookies she'd happily bake for her friends. Like Pavlov's dog, my mouth started watering at the thought of all these goodies appearing, and at the thought of steak! Did I even remember what it tasted like?

"So come on in. Sit yo'self down. It smells in the trailer, but I've set the table for the occasion and we're to have a party."

"Alex, I can't believe you."

She pulled out a chair. "Relax. After your surgery, you

deserve this. I'll mash your steak with the peas, potatoes, and cornbread, so you can sip your dinner through a straw. I even have red wine, good red wine, not the cheap stuff—"

"Alex, what's that smell?"

"This trailer, it's just revolting—"

"No, not the trailer. Something else. Gas."

"What a nincompoop! Gas! I've had this thing broiling ten minutes and couldn't figure out why it wasn't heating up. Of course. I forgot to light the pilot light."

"We can eat outside."

"That's right. It's cleaner out there anyway. Let me just light this thing."

I wasn't thinking. Nor was Alex. My mind was wrapped up in the delicacies of steak, my birthday cards, and John Houle. Absently, I watched Alex kneeling down, opening the oven door, and sticking her head inside to light the pilot hole, where ten minutes of natural gas had been gushing out.

It exploded into flame the second the match was struck. A wall of fire enveloped Alex's face and upper body; jumping back, she fell to the floor, pounding at her hair.

"Alex!" I leaped up and raced to grab a towel to try to put out the flames.

As instantly as it had started, the fire was out. She lay huddled in a ball in the corner, her face wrapped in her arms. I fell beside her, praying she was not badly burned. Taking her hands from her face, she looked up helplessly.

"Mar, my face . . ."

My eyes flooded with tears of relief, for Alex's face was not burned. She was unhurt.

"Oh, Alex!" I cried hoarsely. As she reached for me, I grabbed her, rocking her gently. The skin on her face and arms was miraculously untouched. The only thing affected was her hair.

Alex's luxuriant, long, burnished hair, which she wore sweeping down her back and always proclaimed her best feature, was singed to the chin line. Her wavy bangs were burned to nonexistence. And her eyelashes and eyebrows had disappeared, as had all the hair on her arms.

Suddenly she realized this. "That's what smells so awful—my hair!" Jumping up to race to the mirror, she burst into tears. "Oh my God, Marcy, I look like a freak!"

I smiled wanly. "That makes two of us."

Then came the crying jag. After fifteen minutes or so, Alex regained control and turned to me, squaring her shoulders.

"What idiots we are, Mar. 'Babes in the Woods' as Fitch rightly calls us. Lord, I know I should be thankful it's nothing worse, but I look like a Halloween mask!"

I got up and walked to Alex. She did look frightful, with singed-off hair, no brows or lashes. I went for my brush and scissors (unfortunately all I had on hand was a Swiss army knife), and for an hour I combed and trimmed her hair, or what remained of it. Piles of reeking tresses fell to the floor; fortunately Alex had been blessed with unusually thick hair, and what was left was a peculiar bob of wild, brittle lengths.

I could empathize with Alex's bruised vanity as she mournfully regarded herself in the mirror.

"Between your chin and my hair we make quite a team. Maybe we've been put away up here, out of the civilized world, for a reason."

"I think you may be right."

"What about the steaks?"

"I'm not really hungry any more."

"Nor am I. In fact, I don't ever care if I see steaks again."

Looking back, I suppose the great pity of the evening was that we never ate the luscious hunks of meat. We ended up throwing them away. We also threw out the uncooked cornbread. But we did open the wine. Neither of us usually drank much alcohol, but tonight we did. For Alex it was warranted; it put her in a much better frame of mind. Between us we finished the bottle. The following day we were both left with resounding headaches, and neither of us was in any shape to weather the hot sun and look for hours through binoculars.

So we did the only sensible thing. We took the day off, and slept off our misery in the shade of the healing, crooning ponderosa and piñon pines. Arthur never told. And two hapless casualties of wilderness living dealt with their disfigurements privately, greatly soothed by the peace of the mountains, which never judge people on how they look, how successful or fashionable they are, or aren't in our cases. For this reason, I always love the wilderness. In my opinion, there is no better place to heal a wounded spirit than the outdoors. It gives strength and solace to all, even people with no hair or those who look like Santa Claus.

Chapter Twenty

"THIS OVERGROWN BRUSH is a helluva mess. This job will take more than we bid for, Fitch."

Mr. Fitch demurred. "I agree the area is . . . rather unsuitable for the hundred people we envision, but the most crucial thing right now is toilets."

"Yeah. Toilets. You're right. Folks on tour need toilets."

"Will you have everything done in time?"

"Naturally. We'll rush it through. Hasn't anybody been here since the road got done?"

"Just these girls, this summer."

"Yeah, that's right. I forgot about the per-grines."

I immediately found distasteful the way the contractor spit out the word "peregrines." It sounded like pear-greens, some sort of exotic vegetable. And the talk of the development of Chimney Rock was difficult to hear; it meant the end of the peace and solitude that I had grown to love on the mountain.

Fitch had high hopes for "Phase One," as he proudly referred to it. Presently his plans were restricted somewhat because of the falcons, but he was determined to do all he could within his legal limits. He'd hired a contractor and crew of ten workers for a one week job to prepare the area for a few "test runs" of tourists, an experiment that had been agreed upon by Fitch and Barry Layne. The workmen would clear out and enlarge the parking area and construct a rock wall around it. Fitch also instructed them to widen the trails to the Anasazi ruins, clean out the late summer wildflowers, mountain mahogany and serviceberry bushes that graced the paths now, install several pit toilets at key locations, and, if time permitted, put in metal safety rails around the dropoff at the top, where Alex and I had our lookout. The work was scheduled to begin the week of August 14, when Barry Layne felt the eyrie would no longer be in danger and the fledglings would be old enough to take care of themselves. Of course Barry didn't realize the full situation with regard to Albert. The scientific benefit, Barry felt, to allowing a few selected tours was that I could observe the peregrines' reactions to the commotion, which in theory would aid us in the preparation of our management plan.

Personally, I wasn't wild about the idea. I wished the tours could be put off for another month. But Mr. Fitch feared that after Labor Day people would go home and the chance to show off his peak would be lost. He nagged at Barry and won, not at the expense of Albert, we hoped.

"I will begin leading the tours the week of August 21st," Mr. Fitch explained to the contractor, who was a small, wiry man with rippling forearms and an unshaven face. His taut build looked fully capable of hoisting a load of bricks or stack of four by sixes effortlessly. "I have five lined up already," Fitch went on, "with people knocking down my door."

"What in hell do they hope to see up here?"

"To see?"

"There's nothing here but bugs, cheatgrass, and some beat up old stone piles."

"Anasazi artifacts. As for the condition of the place, that will change. We will have our tourist center, concession stands, the motel and trailer park, and, something Mesa Verde doesn't have, a gondola."

"A what?"

"Gondola. Tramway of the sky. From down there in the valley to all the way up here. Several thousand feet."

"Why didn't you say so? That will snazz this place up."

"Our holdup, of course is that we haven't been granted permission."

"Why not?"

He whispered, "Because of the peregrines."

"I don't believe it! Some dumb birds?"

"There are those that think the birds are quite important." Mr. Fitch glanced my way. "And we in the government believe in the principle of multiple use. As with all things of merit, these things take time."

"Yeah," the contractor snickered, flexing his hands. "Time. That's something we have too much of around here."

Was it taking too much time to decide the proper level of use and management for Chimney Rock? The problems involved in such decisions, which on the surface perhaps look simple, are in fact highly complex. Millions of dollars and our quality of life hinge on the answers. The most popular solution is the one Mr. Fitch mentioned, the philosophy of "multiple use," a catch-all phrase to describe a compromise that results from bargaining among various interests with different wants and needs. Unfortunately, wildlife, having no voice of its own, usually has the least bargaining power and too often is seen as an expendable item, since it returns the smallest profit. Or does it?

Worldwide, hundreds of scientists point to statistics, some pretty frightening, that show how wildlife and plants play vital roles in our well-being. Recently, some renowned scientists have declared that the crisis of species extinction is a threat to civilization second only to the threat of thermonuclear war. Stanford biologist Paul Ehrlich writes that human beings are destroying and depleting the capital of the planet accumulated over hundreds of thousands to millions of years.

An exaggeration? Some people consider it so. But that is because what we are losing is so difficult to see, with our focus on the short term. We can immediately recognize the economic benefits of a dam, a coal-burning plant, or a tourist development. But we can't watch ecosystems daily, each minute, benefit mankind by recycling nutrients for plants we depend on for food and construction materials, by slowly creating soils, by recycling our wastes, and by maintaining and cleansing the air we breathe and the water we drink. These processes are vital to life, but they proceed wordlessly and without fanfare. What we can see are the results when these things go haywire, when man steps in and unwittingly upsets the fine tuning, opening Pandora's box.

Consider Ethiopia. In years past, catastrophic famine has killed thousands of people, and it most assuredly will again in the future. Why? Because man has cut down entire rain forests, creating a cycle that destroys the food people need for sustenance. In 1935, trees covered 30 percent of the land area of Ethiopia. Today they cover only 3 percent. Five hundred thousand acres of forest are cut each year, with a subsequent loss of one hundred and fifty thousand acres to overgrazing and erosion. The result is that, with the trees gone and the soil eroded, the once fertile land withers and becomes a desert where nothing will grow, a land depleted of its life-giving nutrients.

What had this to do with Chimney Rock, Arthur, Leopold, and Albert? Their situation was a variation on the same theme:

seemingly conflicting interests vying for a limited resource. It is a dilemma repeated throughout the world, though in different ways and with different results. The core of the problem is destruction of habitat. It ranges from overgrazing to the destructive properties of acid rain to the filling of wetlands to overdevelopment of coastal systems to bad forestry practices. The price we pay is the reduction of biological diversity. If diversity insures stability, a repeatedly proven ecological concept, then the lack of it, for example in areas restricted to monocultures, means inevitable shake-up of the ecosystem. Though no one can say how severely this will affect us, we do know that somewhere along the line we will feel the loss, in insidious as well as urgent ways.

As a scientist, I was searching for answers. Oftentimes, the more I learn, the more confused I become. To study ecology means to feel despair, but it is also to know the beauty and intricacy of life and to feel hope. I am buoyed by the fact that the United States is a world leader in attempting to curtail habitat destruction.

This is easily recognizable in work with the peregrines. Congress, in acknowledging that the federal government itself is involved in many forms of development, wisely added a provision to the 1973 Endangered Species Act that calls for the designation of "critical habitats" that surround the breeding sites of endangered species. The law requires federal agencies to try to ensure that any actions they fund do not threaten the existence of an endangered species.

It was on this limb that we all stood together: Mr. Fitch, Barry Layne, Alex and I, Arthur and his offspring, and the whole community of this rural Colorado region. There was no single "right" solution; it all hinged on whether one considered short-term or long-term ramifications. And how long was

[139]

long-term? We had a few facts, a melange of options from strip mining to tourist centers to a wildlife sanctuary, and a jumbled mess of hot-collar opinions, one of which was vociferously relayed by the contractor and his men.

The contractor never quit enjoying calling Alex and me fools for doing what we were doing. It disturbed neither of us, for the more we got to know him, the less desirable a character we found him to be. I was bothered far more by his friendly way of invading our trailer at inopportune times, usually when we were preparing dinner or transcribing notes.

He came often. Helping himself to a chair, he sat so close we could smell whatever he'd last had to eat. It didn't help to pull away for he only edged closer, sometimes even reaching out to touch Alex or me on the arm when making a point.

We tried to make excuses to leave at these times, but often he trapped us with "facts" about the tourist center. Our most unpleasant visit was when he came up alone one afternoon to check conditions before his men arrived.

"Your birds can't compete with how long these plans have been in the works," he said, leaning over to see what we were doing. He was carrying papers and shoved a pile under Alex's nose.

"Look here. It says the first sketches of the development were done in 1940, long before you were born. Here it says in 1970 the excavation and stabilization of the ruins started."

"That's nice," commented Alex, disinterested.

He ran a stubby finger down the page, stopping by the year 1971. "Designation of Chimney Rock Archeological Area by the Secretary of Agriculture. How about that! That's when this road was built, and now we're here, and we are the beginning." He paused, looking around the trailer. "That where you sleep, that bunk bed over there?"

We ignored his question.

"Day after day watching per-grines must get boring. You girls need a little excitement."

"We have plenty, thanks."

"No, no, I mean it. We shoot hawks where I come from. The only good hawk is a dead hawk. Why do you write all this stuff?" he asked, picking up a pile of our notes.

"Please, we have these pages in order."

"Pages and pages of . . . what? When the hawks go to the bathroom?" he laughed. "Sure is nothing to do here now. You girls stay up here all alone? I'll bet you have boyfriends. They visit you." He winked a snapping black eye at me.

"No we don't!"

"Oh come on. You can tell me. I can keep a secret. Those Forest Service boys come up here often. I know all about you modern city girls. I read just the other day about a woman, twenty-three years old, who was raped seven times by a man that climbed into her apartment. She asked for it though. She was living alone. Course she let him in. Somewhere in Chicago. Then there was this lady, fifty or so, who got beat up. Beat up bad. They came in with masks. Raped her and beat her. Tied her down—"

"I really don't care to hear about it. If you'll excuse us, Alex and I must be getting back to the lookout."

"She was living alone, just like you are. You've got a neat setup here. Bookshelves, kitchen, dressers—"

"I'm afraid you must leave now; we have to lock the door," I said coldly.

"Lock the—up here? You're a funny one! What's to protect up here? All right, I get the hint. But I'll be back next week. Yes," he said, chuckling to himself, "I'll be back."

Chapter Twenty-One

EVEN MY VIVID imagination did not prepare me for the jolt the contractors brought to our usual placid life on the mountain. For two and a half weeks, the workmen descended upon the wilderness with a discordance similar to the advent of modern television among a community of aborigines. Tranquility and solitude were gone; in their place were chainsaws and construction, dust and debris. And people. People everywhere.

Fitch, in his haste to get going with the nine scheduled tours he had planned, moved up the dates of the visits, which only exacerbated the problem. Now the contractor and his crew tripped over tourists as well as us and our gear, and the peregrines did not always approve.

Wild peregrine falcons, since time immemorial used to being reigning monarchs in their own domain, find such confusion a threat and an aggravation. Arthur's reactions ranged from leaving the vicinity outright to hovering above scanning the mess to screeching his displeasure from the eyrie and, on occasion, to actual aerial displays of defense.

After several days of this, the tiercel must have found himself in something of a dilemma: these people refused to take the hint like eagles and owls did; they didn't go away; nothing Arthur could do seemed to dampen man's continual encroachment. The people didn't act like Alex and me, talking softly and moving slowly, taking time to gain trust by becoming predictable objects. They appeared at all hours during the day, going through all sorts of odd maneuvers. They were not understandable and, therefore, not safe.

Amidst the confusion, I found myself thankful for one thing—it was nearly the end of the peregrine falcon nesting season. Earlier in the summer, Arthur's behavior would have been even more volatile, and the threat that he might abandon the nest and nestlings would have been a real danger. Desertion of peregrine eyries usually results from prolonged, repeated disturbances that keep the birds from their nests.

The sheer number of people hammering, sawing, and shouting added to the peregrines' stress, and when the crew congregated within a half mile of the eyrie, the tiercel often became so hesitant to leave the cliff that he stuck to the Rock like a shop-window mannequin, not hunting or eating, and staying in that position until several hours after the people had left for the afternoon. This could have been a serious problem if the fledglings were not nearly self-sufficient.

The endangered California condors, even more sensitive than peregrines, will stay away from their eggs or young all day and night if even one man exposes himself within five hundred yards of their eyrie at a critical time of the day.

Albert and Leopold each had his own method of dealing with the strain. Initially, I think neither one of them knew enough to be afraid, for at first they reacted as if nothing had changed, continuing to practice their stoops and spins, their hunting skills, and still taking time out to play together and to explore the surrounding countryside. But as time went on and the people did not go away, the fledglings became more suspicious. Leopold's reaction was to spend increasingly more time away from the cliff; Albert stuck near his father and later went into hiding on the other side of the Rock, which created a new problem.

From the lookout it was impossible to see Albert when he was around the cliff, which forced Alex and me to split up, with Alex volunteering to hike to a new observation post two hundred meters north of the Rock, on the opposite face. The absurd decree that we be denied use of walkie-talkies was still in effect; therefore, we were forced to devise another method of communication.

We came up with a splendid new plan, or so we thought until we actually put it to use. It was a signal pantomime that could be seen and relayed from a distance. The moves were rather unusual, considering the information we had to convey, but they worked perfectly to alert us to the falcon's whereabouts.

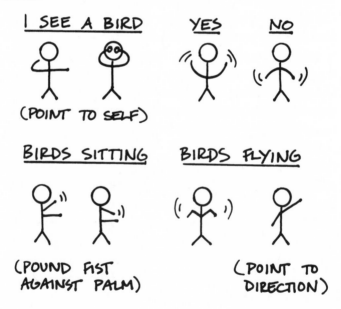

Alex, at her recording post, blended with the groves of ponderosa pines north of Chimney Rock and could hardly be seen by the untrained observer. I, then, was left alone to jump about on the cliff edge for seemingly no apparent reason. Quickly the situation became embarrassing, for the workmen were awed by my behavior, which resembled someone taken to fits.

When at last everyone left at the close of the day, Alex and I walked the trails alone, assessing the damage done to the once pristine mountain. Now, on either side of the trail, lay heaps of piñon pine, mountain mahogany, and serviceberry bushes whacked down by machetes and chainsaws, punishing them for rooting within five feet of the "center line." The newly expanded parking area was being transformed into a work of modern art, with the wall of rocks being painted brown for "naturalness."

Now they were working on toilets. The first potty was erected at the trailhead, only a few hundred feet from our trailer, which was convenient. The second was erected on the top, by the scenic overlook. Curiously, this outhouse was a "two-seater," and the view, facing the canyon, was breathtaking. This, I supposed, was the Forest Service's way of showing a little bit of romance.

As soon as the first toilet was in, Fitch brought up his hordes of tourists. Nothing he had intimated had prepared me for the shock of 148 people spewing forth from several tour buses to descend upon the ruins. I had envisioned a group of ten people, maybe fifteen, but to Fitch's way of thinking, it seemed, 148 meant a "small" group.

I had little say, as this was an experiment and Mr. Fitch was at last in his element, having elected himself tour director. His quiet voice was transmitted over a portable megaphone, and from several hundred yards away I could hear him rounding up his covey to explain the glorious reign of the Anasazis, evidenced by their ruins, the future of which was "uncertain due to the presence of a nest of peregrine falcons."

If that was meant to garner sympathy and support for his position, it backfired, for much to Mr. Fitch's amazement and distress, people began slipping away from him to explore the area for themselves. One by one they filtered up to the lookout to see the peregrines for themselves. Within an hour after tours had begun, I was swarmed by tourists asking questions about the birds. Perched as I was eight feet above them, I had a captive audience and the awkward sensation of being an evangelist who didn't know what to do with her burgeoning flock of disciples, who were mesmerized by my dance to the falcons. Mr. Fitch was rightfully annoyed, emitting silently through stares that this must be all my fault, that I was doing something sinister (especially the gyrating) to bring on the tourists' behavior. Frustrated, he clucked his band into order, dragging it away from the top, back to the buses.

Only one tour stands out in my memory as exceptional, and it was due to the singular character involved and to the fact that she asked Fitch not to accompany her, preferring to go it alone. Looking like a western tanager in springtime plumage, the seventyish woman arrived at the top with her nephew and his bride to see the falcons.

All she said was that her name was Fawcett, Mrs. Fawcett. It wasn't until much later that I learned she was *the* Mrs. Fawcett of the prestigious Fawcett Publishing Company, a multimillion dollar publishing house started by her late husband. But who she was didn't matter. She stood at the cliff edge wearing a blue denim suit, highlighted by several chic touches such as sprigs of juniper tucked into her collar, a golden yellow sunflower peeking from her breast pocket, a red bandana on her head. Strapped to her hip belt by a silver chain was an elegantly carved wooden cane that she could retract at the touch of a button.

After nearly two weeks of consistent denigration from the contractors and gawking from most of the tourists, Alex's and my spirits were lifted by her surprising knowledge of birds and wildlife and her vociferous commendation of the work we were doing. As she tried to speak over the howling wind, she tapped her staff like a gavel, motioning for us to stand closer.

"Now that I've seen this for myself, after all these years, I realize there is only one thing that must be done. You must save this land." At the end of each phrase, she pounded her cane for punctuation. "You must save it for the wildlife, for your peregrines. Shame on Fitch, letting all these people up here when he knows it disturbs them so. *I* shouldn't even be here!"

"At least you're one, not one hundred and forty."

The cane tap, tap, tapped. "It's a disgrace. I shall have a chat with him tomorrow. This area should remain pristine as it is now, unspoiled, for the peregrine's sakes.

"Once people are allowed to trample all over this crystalline area, as they're doing now, nothing will be left. How well I know. I have my own hundred-or-so acre retreat deep in the San Juan Mountains. The one season I allowed the public in, my wildlife was frightened away, my trails strewn with garbage. Now, in an arrangement I have with the Forest Service, I let them walk on one trail, and one trail only, and even so, every morning after breakfast I still must hike down with my wicker basket to retrieve the mess people leave."

Her nephew, a tall, fit man in his forties draped with expensive camera gear, smiled to himself.

"Michael thinks I'm a doddering old fool—don't you?—but Canny knows."

"Canny?" I asked.

"Short for Canfield, of course. Canny is my personal guardian and roommate. He is also a crow. I must say, he is smarter than any six-year-old child, and the best watchdog I've ever had, and I've thirteen now. He understands every word I say. If I hear someone coming up to the main house I say, 'Canfield, my pet, who is it?' and he walks to the door, crouches down, and peeks at whoever is coming. If it's a stranger, he cries for the maids and the dogs. If the dogs are roaming about the grounds, he continues squabbling until they arrive."

Albert flew out from the cliff after a purple dragonfly,

missed, saw the four people standing at the lookout, and darted for safety.

"There he is!" exclaimed Mrs. Fawcett. "Michael, did you see that lovely thing fly? Such grace and elan."

(Elan? Albert?)

"I've always dreamed of seeing a peregrine, and now I have. Children, what are your names?"

"Marcy—Marcy Cottrell, and I'm Alex Porter," said Alex, smiling.

"Well, Miss Marcy Cottrell and Miss Alex Porter, I know there's been lots of talk in town about the terrible things you are doing. But I want you to know, the people who say it are fools. Now that I've seen you for myself, I see you are delightful young women, and so what if you're unpopular! Being unpopular isn't so bad. Being untrue is. I've been unpopular many times in my life, and it hasn't hurt me at all. I'm still included in all the important functions, and I've been everywhere and seen everything."

Just at this moment, a horsefly, coming from who knows where, as horseflies usually preferred the habitat nearer the river bottom, flew up in the wind and swirled around her head. As I reached up to swat it away, Mrs. Fawcett raised her arms in alarm.

"No, no, dear! Let the fly go!"

By its own accord, it droned off to some new territory, probably scouting for some deer in the thicket.

"I deplore killing anything, dear, especially flies. My dear late-husband's name was Buzz, you see, and never could I hurt anything that buzzed. Why, they remind me of him."

Pulling down on the brim of the red bandana she had tied to her head, Mrs. Fawcett cast a fey glance at the cliff where Albert had hidden himself.

[149]

"Yes, it is a bit hard having people despise you for living for something you believe in. But that is the way of the world. We're run by greed and selfishness." She pulled out the juniper from her collar and took a whiff. "Isn't this lovely. Just smelling it reminds me of the important things in life. We must always hold onto our ideals. For me it's a place called Born Lake, for you it's your falcons. Pin your ideals on those falcons. Those ideals won't die, and in them there's power."

"Auntie, we must be going."

"Yes, Canny will be upset that I've been gone this long." Mrs. Fawcett patted each of us fondly on the shoulder. "Remember, believe in those flying peregrines. Then, whatever happens, you'll be prepared."

"Prepared for what?" laughed her nephew.

Mrs. Fawcett scowled at him. "Michael, you'll never understand. Even though I've tried drumming these things into you since you were a child."

She turned one last time to face me, her eyes the color of tiny blue juniper berries. "I think you know what I'm talking about. You'll be prepared."

Chapter Twenty-Two

WHEN THE TOURISTS weren't at the lookout, the workmen were, readying it for more tourists and discussing the positioning of the safety rails the Forest Service wanted to be up by next summer. The unrelenting presence of human beings soon transformed the scenic setting of Chimney Rock into a dust-swirling pitstop. For the peregrines, this at times acted like tightening a screw on an already taut situation. Albert stayed hidden, Leopold soon joined him, and Arthur, when he was home, hunched his powerful shoulders against his bullet-shaped head and repeatedly rocketed over Chimney Rock.

For all Arthur's effort, however, he continued to reap only sneers. Still undaunted by the end of the second week, the tiercel began transferring his aggression to the innocent ravens, attacking them and creating in them such terror that they soon did not dare to show their heads from the cliff at any time the contractors were present.

The agreement between the U.S. Forest Service and the Colorado Division of Wildlife clearly stated that the workmen could proceed with limited construction in mid-August, under the common assumption that peregrine falcons will tolerate human activity near the eyrie late in the nesting season when the nestlings have fledged. But what we were observing disintegrated the theory that the peregrine family unit begins breaking up when fledglings reach the young age of five to six weeks. At least for Albert and Leopold. The two fledglings were on the edge of thirteen weeks, and Arthur was still feeding them. The tiercel's defensive response was still apparent. To me it was becoming more evident that to release throngs of tourists or construction crews earlier than late August was premature.

I could already hear the rebuttal to that stand: peregrines were known to reside on skyscrapers in major cities, where thousands of people pressed below them, so why couldn't these birds put up with a little noise late in the summer? But there was a difference—a difference in individual peregrines. These birds of Chimney Rock were wild. They preferred the wilderness and were highly territorial, which meant in ornithological terms that they would put on a show of defense if disturbed by something as far as a mile away from the cliff. Less territorial falcons will let an intruder, bird or man, pass within one hundred to five hundred yards of their nest. Not Arthur, and not the majority of peregrine falcons. As much as the city skyscraper peregrines, feasting on pigeons and starlings, capture the reporter's limelight, these instances are only occasional departures from the remote, cliff-nesting adaptation of the species.

I feared this little bit of news would be unwelcome to developers and many members of the local community and also to the contractor and workmen, whose hostility over the closure of Chimney Rock was clearly growing stronger as they neared the end of their tenure. This was uncomfortably apparent their final days at Chimney Rock, when their work kept them concentrated at the top, where I was. I could sense the imminence of an eruption between us, one I dearly hoped to avoid. Possibly it never would have happened if it hadn't been for the untimely loss of one ball-peen hammer.

On the contractor's final day, one of the workmen, a tall, burly fellow whose shoulders told of years of heavy construction work, showed off to the others his mastery of baton-twirling, using his heavy and expensive hammer as the baton, flinging it high into the air, catching it the second before it was about to plunge over the drop-off. The men, riveted by his performance, cheered him, setting up such a racket that Arthur flew off, which unfortunately made the workman take his eyes off his hammer for an instant, resulting in the tool slipping through his fingers to fall out of sight.

"Damnit!" the man barked. "I'm not climbing down there to get that thing back!"

His cronies laughed, chiding him for showing off in the first place and secondly for letting a bird interfere with his concentration.

The response only angered the man further. "It's the damn bird's fault!"

"Well, Burt, think of it this way, you won't need your hammer anyway after this week."

My stomach was beginning to churn as several of the workmen looked up to grimace at me.

"It's not the bird's fault, Burt," said one. "Put the blame where the blame's due: biologists."

My note-taking suddenly became extremely consuming. "Biologists are putting us out of a job. They're government subsidized and we're not. Well, not usually," he added under his breath. "And these penguins here probably live better than you and I! Think the government's got things screwed somewhere?"

"My tax money going to penguins?"

I sighed. The all-too-familiar headache was coming on.

"Like hell it is!" he went on. "My money ain't going to penguins! I've got bills to pay and a wife and kids to feed and I'll be damned if I'm going to support penguins too. Especially when I'm out of a job."

I could see the repugnant crew leader, whom Alex and I had successfully avoided for the entire week, pushing his way to the front of the fracas, smiling to himself with a satisfied expression, like he was just about to enjoy a full and luscious meal. Scratching his mustached face, he put his hand on the workman's shoulder.

"What's going on here, fellas?"

"Hank was pouring out his usual crap that my money pays this dame to watch penguins."

I writhed inside at the lead contractor's smug countenance. "But it does, Burt. That's this little girl's job."

"What the hell! If that's true, then all I can say is penguins better taste good!"

"Let's try an experiment," said another voice chiming in. "Let's see just how good penguins taste! That bird's close enough to get a real good shot."

"Can't do that," the contractor reprimanded. "This lovely lady biologist will report you, and the government will lock you away."

"Let it try! I have no use for a government that says a nest of penguins is more important than I am. That's ridiculous! They got it all fouled up somewhere when a damn girl gets paid to sit around on her ass all day while the rest of us dumbshits work!"

All of a sudden the lead contractor turned on the sympathy. It was obvious what he was up to, and I despised him for it. "Didn't your wife just get laid off of her job, Burt?" he asked gently. "What will you do now, Burt? Now that the job's over.

How will you put food on the table?"

"I'll wring a penguin's neck, by golly. Wrap it round and round like a chicken bound for the dining table —"

"Not penguins, Burt, you're forgetting. How can you blame a poor, innocent penguin," muttered the contractor. "You're putting the blame in the wrong place." He gave me a pointed look.

The workman followed his eyes. "Aw, she's just a kid."

"Kid?" said the contractor, appraising me. "Why she's a grown woman—a lady biologist. She knows what she's doing. And she's got one hell of a good set up . . . at your expense watching Pinocchio the Penguin."

I'd had enough. "Look, I'm sorry you feel the way you do, but I work hard too, and the penguins—I mean peregrines— deserve the right to be here, to exist, as much as you and I do. They serve a purpose."

It was the wrong thing to say. Ten pairs of eyes glowered up at me. "What purpose?"

I was stuck now. "Well, they are predators, like we are. What happens to them affects us. They provide . . . provide diversity." I was fumbling for words, flailing in the pervading spirit of their antagonism, and they knew it. What on earth could the ecological concept of diversity mean to them, and especially at this moment? What could I say to set matters right?

("You'll be prepared," Mrs. Fawcett had said. How come I didn't feel at all prepared?)

"They are a unique species," I began again.

"Cut the crap, lady."

"The bird didn't make you lose your hammer. You lost it because you dropped it yourself over the cliff! The birds are only defending their nest."

"You listen here, girlie," interrupted the contractor. "We didn't ask for these penguins. And we didn't ask for you. You environmentalists are all alike. Claiming what you're doing is for man, but you don't know nothing about how the other half lives." The man spit on the ground and covered it up with dust kicked from his boot. "So take the hint. Take it before it's too late."

From the corner of my eye, I saw a hefty workman bend over to pick up something. Giving him room, the contractor stood back.

"See this rock, girlie?" the man hollered angrily. "It's just the right size to break a window, or to bust a bird's skull. Watch."

Leaning back for momentum, the man with bulging arms hurled the rock toward Chimney Rock. Silently it fell down, down, down the canyon to be swallowed up in the black trees below.

"That one is for your birds. For your precious penguins, lady."

Chapter Twenty-Three

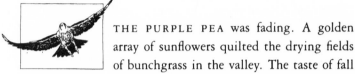 THE PURPLE PEA was fading. A golden array of sunflowers quilted the drying fields of bunchgrass in the valley. The taste of fall brushed against my lips with every breeze that played with the red-blushed serviceberry leaves and ripening seeds of Gambel oak and Douglas fir. Climbing the slopes of the encircling San Juan Range, saffron patches of aspen were strewn about like beach blankets thrown on the sand on a busy day. The cool, crisper air quickened the blood, as birds began to cluster, in the foreshadowing of their migration.

Fall had come to Chimney Rock. Subtle at first but more apparent every day, the signs of encroaching winter had all the animals scurrying about, like they had awakened from the lingering dog days of summer, when food and cover were rich and abundant, to the harsh fact that the business of survival was soon to be upon them. The weekend was over. Monday had come.

For Albert and Leopold, mid-September meant their carefree youth had begun its final chapter. Inevitably, their youthful reliance on forces outside of themselves was tapering off. And this was a good thing; all too abruptly their lives would depend on how well they had mastered the skills that Arthur had so patiently taught them. By the month's end, the family bond that had been the mainstay of their existence would be loosened. Each peregrine would move on, separately, to his wintering grounds far to the south.

This is the most crucial time in a young peregrine's life, when he is about to leave home and must depend upon his own inexperienced hunting ability and poorly developed survival skills. These talents take years to develop; even a one-year-old peregrine is less proficient at the art of hunting than a fully adult bird.

Were Albert and Leopold ready? Leopold was rapidly gaining in self-sufficiency—he was hunting quite professionally now—but I often wondered about Albert. He still liked to stick close to home, to chase Arthur when he sneaked home for a moment's roost, to stir up a rousing game with his sibling when Leopold was in the mood. In flight, I could hardly tell them apart; both were aces of the sky, outmaneuvering every other species born with wings. But as for sheer drive for independence, Albert worried me.

Yet, whether Albert liked it or not, by necessity he would soon be forced to face life alone and to deal with the hardships it would bring him. The statistics proved that. Seventy percent of the peregrine fledglings born this year would die. They would die from starvation, from bullets, from collisions with telephone lines and power poles. Only the more fortunate thirty percent would live to see their first birthday. A lot depended on simple luck. If the fledglings should live through their first winter, the statistical probability of their making it through a second improved dramatically. A peregrine would need to live at least that long to be able to breed; few peregrines mate and raise young until they are at least two years old, and many do not nest until they are three or four. Once again there is a difference in the sexes: wild females generally come into breeding condition earlier, while tiercels rarely breed until three, four, sometimes even five years old.

If a peregrine were favored, he could expect to live for seven or even ten years. In captivity, peregrine falcons have been observed to live to the ripe old age of twenty. But captivity poses far fewer risks than the real, wild world. The chances were slim that both the young falcons I had watched and come to love would make it, though I still prayed they would be among the fortunate minority.

With the peregrines' activity at the eyrie diminishing, I had, looming over my head like a bad dream, two hundred pages of notes that had to be typed for the Division of Wildlife, then analyzed by statistical methods. From these results, Alex and I would draw up recommendations for the Chimney Rock peregrine management plan. But where Alex was a speedy and amiable typist, I am not. Typewriters and I have a serious disagreement; I think faster than I type, and that creates endless frustration. I also dislike being cooped up over a desk for long hours, and in this case the thought of spending a week or more of evenings in town at the Forest Service office (Fitch had kindly donated his personal secretary's typewriter for our use) was decidedly unappealing. However, the results of the work were noteworthy, which drove me to wish to see them in print.

Alex and I had discussed earlier our findings with Pat Waters, and going over them in my mind, I could see again the patterns, which fell into three main categories.

Peregrines and hunting success: Unlike previously suspected, our work showed that the hunting attacks of peregrine falcons were more often than not unsuccessful. After hundreds of hours of observation, we had documented over and over again that it took many tries for a wild falcon to procure its prey. Therefore, a significant portion of a nesting peregrine's day was spent trying to acquire food, for itself and for its young.

Peregrines and hunting areas: Unlike previously suspected, we found that the Chimney Rock peregrines conducted most of their hunting away from the eyrie, many times travelling miles from the cliff to find food. As a result, this would mean that when scientists or developers delineated peregrine hunting areas, they could not always assume that a mere one mile radius around the eyrie would be sufficient.

Presence of man near a peregrine eyrie: We observed that human presence, especially if within a quarter mile of an active peregrine nest, caused the peregrines distress throughout the nesting season. Additionally, we found that peregrine defensive reactions increased proportionally to the number of consecutive days they had been bothered.

It all really boiled down to one thing: for peregrine falcons, the dimensions of critical habitat (food, nesting, and hunting habitat) were greater in size and scope than previously suspected. The old simple rule of thumb used by developers and managers that a mile-wide undisturbed radius around a peregrine eyrie would provide adequate protection was not always viable. In working terms, this meant two things: that the hunting areas of nesting peregrines needed to be defined, then protected, however far away from the eyrie they were, and also that access to a peregrine eyrie should be limited until fledgling peregrines were at least twelve, possibly fifteen weeks old (usually in late August or early September), as parent falcons still actively fed their young until this time.

The scientist in me was pleased to pass on this news; the unpopular young woman, however, felt reluctant. I could foresee hot discussions arising from our summer's research on the falcons—steamy sessions with wide-ranging ramifications. Fitch would be apprehensive; archeological buffs would feel snubbed; tourists would be inconvenienced; Indians would proclaim they were being shut out from what they felt was their land; local promoters would cry foul.

The game now was in the court of politics. With startling clarity, I saw how a biologist's life was probably at most 60 percent science; the rest was politics. And as much as I wished, I could not let myself believe that the Endangered Species Act automatically provided protection for the peregrine above other pressing economic interests. Undoubtedly, our conclusions would affect the proposed archeological development in some fashion and have tentacles reaching out far into the surrounding area. But how much change, how much preservation, would be allowed? How would the community, the county, state, and even the federal government respond to the report?

There was one truth: "answers" only create more questions. No one can say, at least not yet, that coal developments, subdivisions, ski resorts, oil drilling, and wildlife sanctuaries can function side by side. So how does one decide which takes precedence?

Many say the answer must come through science. But as a scientist, I know that we are forced to find answers quickly, sometimes too quickly, with society a jump ahead, trying to fit or force what scientists are only just discovering into a scheme that is already in motion.

These thoughts spun about my head on the morning of Saturday, September 16, their lack of precise definition aptly fitting with the unusual, obscuring fog that draped the mountain in a shroud of whiteness. Last night there had been a late-season thunderstorm that seized the mountain and our flimsy trailer, and by dawn everything was wringing wet. At seven o'clock, after grabbing my down jacket, I stood outside to smell the heightened fragrance of the dripping evergreen needles. Oceans of mist filled up the valleys below; a warming sun, just beginning to slip up behind the Rock and to send slanting, long rays creeping down the trail, set to sparkling the clinging drops of rain on the red fescue grass.

I felt weighted this morning, tired, with the beginnings of a headache caused by the low pressure system. Yes, it was a perfectly horrible day to spend hunched over a typewriter, ruining your eyes trying to decipher piles of notes written in longhand with a pencil. (Field biologists always take notes in pencil, since ink will run in the rain.)

But I had little choice in the matter, for the notes were already packed, and once again we were nearly out of food and water and desperately in need of flashlight batteries. Both our flashlights had died, and we had no lantern. Ten hours of uninterrupted work at the typewriter with no one to disturb us (employees vanished from the Forest Service office on Saturdays and Sundays) would put us several days ahead. That the office was locked on weekends presented no problem: the same key that opened the Chimney Rock gate and our airstream trailer also opened the door to the Forest Service main office.

Unceasingly, and rather idiotically, for our mistakes far outweighed our progress, Alex and I worked until eleven o'clock that night, driving at the blasted typewriters until we were bleary-eyed with fatigue and almost not speaking after hours of arguing over what we had written in our less decipherable notes. Careening back to the mountain in a semi-somnolent state, the tail end of the truck sliding and flailing all over the slick road like a dying, spawning salmon who cared only to reach its destination, we at last approached the trailer as the rain began to fall again.

Climbing out of the vehicle, I felt the tight-wrapped night—even more oppressive than the morning. A night of no moon or stars, no yipping coyotes, gloomy with the residual effects of a late afternoon thunderstorm and the threat of a new one. But presently I couldn't care less; I only wanted bed.

Rain spilled down the back of my neck as I groped my way through the dark, feeling for the rusted, metal door. We had forgotten the flashlight batteries again. These were the times when I yearned for a yellow, flickering lantern or even a mediocre thing like a stark light bulb dangling from a string, to call me home, to lure me enticingly inside—any simple light would do—to act like a friendly beacon in the wilderness. It was too late tonight for a fire and far too wet. Whimsically I pondered, where is the maid waiting for us with a hot slice of pie, a cup of slowly brewed coffee, elegantly laid out on a table decorated with an Irish lace tablecloth and cloth napkins? Funny, I hadn't thought of cloth napkins for over four months. Somehow tonight they seemed the epitome of luxury. At midnight, fumbling for the door, wiping the rain from my face, all I wanted was cloth napkins.

"You spilled, Mar."

"What?"

"You must have spilled oatmeal or something all over the floor when you left. It's a gritty mess."

"I didn't spill oatmeal. I didn't *eat* oatmeal for breakfast!" I tripped into the trailer behind Alex, unable to see anything.

"Rice, then. It's all over the counter. Really, you should have picked up before you left!"

"Alex, I did not spill rice or oatmeal or any such thing. How it got over everything, I haven't the faintest. And I don't care. I'm going to bed."

Passing Alex, my boots crunched over what felt like a layer of spilled split peas. My knee ran into an opened drawer as my hand brushed over the top of the cabinet, which was covered with something, something like dust, or flour.

"It was your responsibility to remember the batteries, Mar."

"Don't be ridiculous!" I said, banging into the dresser again. "Why is it always my fault? And why is all your stuff on the floor? Alex, your underpants! How utterly disgusting . . . they're all over the floor!"

Kicking them aside in the pitch darkness, I inched forward, scuffling my feet like an old woman of ninety, at last feeling the bunkbed, where I leaned my tired head in exhaustion. The sheet, that ghastly plastic nuisance, felt split. Dreamily, I ran my hand down the bed, now awakening more by the second. No, not split, slit—ripped up. Jagged edges of plastic cut at my fingers.

Someone had been in here.

Almost instantly Alex cried out that the gritty substance on the floor was pieces of broken glass from smashed bottles.

"Dammit! Something's happened here and we don't even have a lousy candle!"

Pawing my way, I patted for the familiar possessions—our sleeping bags, toiletries, jackets. None of them was here. Throwing open the closet, I groped unsuccessfully for my camera, money, binoculars, camping gear, and the $1500 police radio. The cupboard was bare. Only a stray bit of down from a pillow wafted by my nose.

Alex, always the cool Texan, was fighting to stay calm. "Damn, damn, damn," she cried, slapping her fist on the dresser. "Oh, damn."

The lonely spitting of rain outside picked up its intensity, the sound reverberating in the hollow, metal trailer like gunshots going off. Someone had been in here, and someone had used force, intentional, menacing force, to vandalize our home and our lives.

Chapter Twenty-Four

AFTER A SLEEPLESS NIGHT, the light at dawn revealed a ransacking so loathsome and incongruous with the glorious sunrise that it was difficult to comprehend. The sun rose just as it always did, squeezing between the two large pinnacles that formed Chimney Rock, glowing red, then orange, then golden yellow, and finally popping over the top and casting everything with citrine luminescence. But what it saw was a different place, a once pastoral scene now marked with the scourge of man and a fetid taste of his meanness.

Alex and I made a cursory list of the things taken, which amounted to just about everything of value and much that was not—cameras, radios, binoculars, spotting scopes and lenses, sleeping bags, back packs, the Coleman stove and our camp stoves, tents, ground covers, water bottles, jackets, hats, change, Coleman fuel—all the camping gear that we relied on down to the last compass. And then the strange things: the thermometer and anamometer we used for recording temperatures and wind speed, our books, our photographs, both professional and personal, and what we had left behind of our notes. (I refrained from thinking about what the extent of the disaster would have been if we hadn't had most of the research with us in town—four months worth of data down the drain.) Also gone, strangely, were cereal, canned food, and, most surprisingly, our cooler of dead birds.

Someone had wiped us clean. Yet somehow that wasn't what bothered me. What was worse, far worse, was the vandalism. The broken glass; the foodstuffs—what remained of them— ripped apart and strewn everywhere; the jug of water poured over the counters; our clothes ransacked. But the lookout hit me hardest. In the morning we discovered that the boards that had supported it were over the cliff.

No, this was too shocking and violent to register meaning in my naive, trusting brain. People didn't act like this, not here; in big cities perhaps, but not in the wild places. No, it didn't make sense at all, and I had to pinch myself at intervals to make certain I wasn't dreaming the whole thing.

Walking around the mountaintop with its well-loved trails, I found myself looking over my shoulder, being accompanied by a new prickling sensation along my spine.

Remembering the awful days after Jenny's killing, with deep relief I saw that Arthur and his band were unharmed. The three peregrines perched as silhouettes on the backlighted rock, waiting to take flight for breakfast, or perhaps they had just had their meal; I was too late at the top to tell. But those three lone black figures suddenly stood for all that was safe and unruffled, though I couldn't stop to watch them now, even though they were the only things that seemed to have any sensibility.

We interrupted Fitch at his quiet Sunday breakfast. Feasting on scrambled eggs and sausages, sitting outside on the sunny patio, he frowned as his wife directed us his way. He looked as if a bucket full of cold water had just been dashed across his psyche, and with his napkin in hand dabbing his lips, he stood up.

"Girls, you could have called first."

"We have some bad news, Mr. Fitch."

"You broke the typewriter."

"No, not that, our trailer—"

"You locked yourselves out of the trailer and have lost the key. I informed you from the beginning there would be only one key in your possession, that it was your responsibility to guard it, making certain you kept it on your person at all times."

"Mr. Fitch, we have been vandalized."

The words failed to register at first; Mr. Fitch's face wore the same bland expression, as if we had merely said "we ran out of gas," but then a look of rising alarm blanched his jowls and his eyes widened.

"What did you say?"

"We have been vandalized. We arrived home late last night after a long day in town, found everything torn apart, everything that remained that is, since most was stolen."

"I'm not reading you."

With the napkin, Mr. Fitch dabbed his brow, accidentally spreading a yellowish wash of egg across his forehead.

I began again. This time I tried being more graphic in the description, and reaching behind him for his chair, Mr. Fitch slouched down, clenching and reclenching the napkin.

He muttered something to himself and suddenly jumped up. "Government property!"

I stared blankly.

"They . . . they . . . these criminals, vandalized government property!"

"Yes, they did, but they also took all of our scientific equipment, personal belongings, and—"

"They went up there . . . through the locked gates . . . and harmed government property. Agnes, get me the phone

book! Yes, what I must do is call the F.B.I. This is a case for
the F.B.I. Desecrated government property. The trailer! That
lovely trailer that I struggled to obtain for you. And now it's
ruined! I should never have assigned it to your job. What else
did you say was vandalized?"

I repeated the list while Fitch dialed the phone. At first he
was unsuccessful getting through, but with the operator's
assistance he reached the F.B.I. office in Durango. They said
they would dispatch an officer right away to meet us at the
Forest Service. Thrusting aside his half-finished breakfast,
Fitch also phoned the state and local police, then raced about
to locate his car keys, which he had misplaced.

"This is a travesty! Think of it! Destroying Forest Service
property . . . and my trailer."

I winced. "And scientific things too. Our notes, we nearly
lost the whole summer's worth of notes, our cameras, scopes,
the cooler of birds."

Fitch stiffened. "Cooler of what?"

"Um . . . birds. For prey analysis," I added quickly. "I've
been collecting them all summer."

"Birds? Dead birds?"

"Yes . . . feathers, things like that. Below the eyrie. Prey
species, for I. D. purposes, you know."

"You had a cooler full of dead birds? Oh, my God. And
you'd been keeping them in my trailer?"

In less than an hour, an F.B.I. agent, the local sheriff, three
state patrolmen, and Pat Waters converged at the Forest Service office. Hands trembling and chattering a mile a minute,
Mr. Fitch unlocked the office door, steering us all inside to his
impeccable office where everything had been neatly put away
for the weekend, even the last stray pencil. As there were not

enough chairs for all of us to sit down, Alex and I stood and were examined by all the authorities, who, aside from Pat, made it seem like we were the criminals about to be interrogated, rather than the helpless victims.

The agent, a tall, spare man with a long, expressionless face and narrow, cadaver-like fingers, silently opened his briefcase and removed a micro tape recorder.

Yawning, he pushed the microphone in front of my nose. "Let's have it in your own words first."

I recounted what had happened, Alex seconded it, and the agent, yawning for a third and fourth time, retrieved another black box from the case.

"You're fingerprinting them?" asked Fitch.

"Uh huh."

"But why? After all, they . . . well, at least Miss Porter is a screened and trusted employee of the Forest Service."

The agent ignored him. "You." He pointed again at me. "Come over here." Grabbing my hand with his thin, bony fingers, he squashed my fingers one by one into the ink pad, then mashed them down on the standardized form where he had printed my name boldly across the top.

"Next!"

Alex, shaking with fatigue and nerves, said sweetly in her high-pitched voice, growing steadily higher all morning, "I don't believe this! This can't have really happened!"

"Well it did, so believe it."

There was commotion coming from the hallway, a troop of people barging into the office, which was surprising for a Sunday, but in my exhaustion—neither Alex nor I had slept for over thirty hours—I rubbed my tired face and eyes with my hands in an effort to stimulate the brain and wake myself up, not caring who was cavalcading inside. Fitch was disrupted by the noise and breathed fast, drumming the desk with his fingers; Alex was nearly in tears; I felt that if I didn't sit down soon I would fall down. The hot, sickly perspiration of mental and physical drain crept under my arms and clutched at my temples; black spots were beginning to swirl before my eyes; saliva was welling up, filling my throat—I was going to lose it.

"Excuse me," Fitch remarked. "All this commotion is unpardonable. Let me shut the door to my office. Yes, what is it you want, Mr. Houle?"

A form, lean and tall, was at the doorway, staring in with disbelief, then concern, then pity. Oh my Lord, the young engineer again. Like a guest who shows up at only the worst times, there he was again, the one person I wanted just now the least to see, and he was here in full rugged stature, just as I was about to throw up.

"The men and I just arrived back from the Mt. Pagosa fire," John explained. "I noticed the . . . the garbage truck outside, and the patrol cars. Just wondered if everything was all right."

"No, everything's not all right. My property has been abused. Now if you'll leave us to our business—"

I was going to sink into a chair. And die. Other firefighting foresters were careening their heads around John to get a look, delighted to see it was us being called on the carpet. It sounded as if *we* had molested the equipment, had been caught red-handed by the police doing something terrible. Of course, we were guilty.

"Awful pretty face you've got there," said one charcoal-faced, bearded man who wiggled his finger at me. "On the warpath, eh? Or have you just been fingerpainting again?"

"Stanley. Can't you boys see we're busy!"

"Sorry, Mr. Fitch."

Stanley moved out of the doorway in poorly controlled hysterics while John remained in place, not laughing, with only concern on his face. I was more than humiliated now. Fingerpainting? What the hell?

Alex leaned aside, whispering, "The ink . . . from the pad . . . you smeared it all over your face."

A white piece of toilet paper was being dangled at me from the doorway by a convulsing forester. Mr. Fitch banged his fist down on the table, "John, will you please retrieve a Kleenex for this girl?"

John disappeared, then returned with a tissue, and a mirthful but not unkind smile.

Had I no pride?

"Mr. Houle, you can go now."

Gently he put the paper in my hand. His dark eyes revealed compassion as he searched my dirty face. Why was he so nice, so damnably handsome?

"You're sure you're okay?" he asked seriously.

Pulling my shoulders erect, I nodded, unable to look him in the eye.

"If you please!" exclaimed Fitch.

John smiled kindly, in calm control, and walked out. The F.B.I. agent, who had been observing the whole interlude with growing impatience, snapped his briefcase shut. "The next step is to drive to the site to look for evidence."

"Yes . . . yes of course. I'll take the van, we can all ride together."

"I'd prefer taking my own vehicle, Mr. Fitch."

Here Alex interjected that no one would get far if they didn't have four-wheel-drive, considering the condition of the road after the weekend thunderstorm.

"That presents a problem," the agent griped. "It means all sign of tracks may be obliterated."

"There must be some tracks!" said Fitch. "Let's hurry before it begins raining again!"

Last night's storm had indeed washed out all sign of tracks, with the exception of our own deeply rutted ones from this morning, which were presently filling in with rivulets of water. The agent sighed and began searching for fingerprints on the trailer door, inside the trailer, and everywhere else the vandals might have left a complete mark. On the sidelines were the patrolmen, Mr. Fitch, Pat, and Alex and I, all of us restrained from interjecting much help, for federal regulations assert that offenses to government property must be handled by federal authorities—disinterested as they may be—which unfortunately ties the hands of local police who may have more at stake.

It was apparent that the agent, who seemed more than ever like a funeral director, with his crane-like neck and indoor pallor, had scant intention of following up on the leads; but what he concluded after an hour's investigation showed he had been listening astutely to the whole picture we portrayed. After some discussion with the state patrolmen and local sheriff, he zeroed in on what he thought was the motive.

"Enemies!" shouted Fitch after hearing the verdict. "How is that possible? These young, innocent women, alone in the wilds far from man—"

"This is more than a case of simple burglary," the agent interrupted dispiritedly. "Consider for a moment the selectivity in the choice of stolen items—books, photographs, notes on the falcons. Someone wanted to frighten these girls. They've accrued enemies because of their research."

"Those damn falcons," growled Fitch. "It's their fault. If they weren't here, none of this would have happened. And never did I believe for a moment women should be involved in this work."

He turned toward me. "I told you from the start I didn't approve of you being on Chimney Rock. Think what could have happened if those criminals had found you here yesterday!"

That was something I wished to refrain from thinking about. I listened as if from a distance to the discussion going on about me, while my thoughts swirled around the bigger picture—the growing unease of the entire region, with factions fighting with one another to promote their own interests—coal mining, power plants, real estate, tourist development, Indians wanting their land back. Like a grumbling volcano long thought inactive but now trembling the ground with life, the virgin four-corners region of Colorado, New Mexico, Utah, and Arizona was facing an inevitable eruption, not now perhaps, but sometime in the future, whereby interests competing over limited but priceless resources would change irrevocably the face of the Southwest.

I felt drained and miserably unhappy that the whole thing should have ended like this. Something had gone wrong along the way. And somehow it was all symbolized in the missing cooler filled with dead birds.

We, and the peregrines, had been caught in the middle, amidst something much bigger than ourselves, yet whose future concerned all of us.

Chapter Twenty-Five

 PEOPLE ARE CONTRARY. Just when you think you have them all figured out, nestled away in neat little categories, they surprise you and turn 180 degrees around to act completely unlike the way you knew they would, thereby baffling you with their complexity and making you realize you never, never can classify them with any kind of certainty. They will only astonish you.

Word about the robbery spread quickly through the local villages while the investigation continued. In less than a week, while Alex and I lived in the displaced luxury of a real Forest Service trailer with six other single women, everyone in town down to the dogcatcher knew the story, with all the particulars, even the underpants.

But the fallout from the incident confounded my sensibilities, for what I expected to happen did not, and what I least anticipated did; it was like having people throw you a birthday party just when you are certain you have not a friend in the world.

I presumed that the local townspeople would cheer at the break up of the scientists' lives at Chimney Rock, a kind of tar and feathering to rid the town of the scourge that kept the area from enjoying its almost guaranteed prosperity. With the birdwatchers gone, I reasoned for them, business could proceed as planned, after only a slight, if distasteful, delay. Now there would be "food on the table for everyone," the local folks on welfare could resume work, jobs would abound, the business leaders could delight in dollar signs dangling before their eyes.

But people are contrary. They did not react as I misjudged they would. The majority of the inhabitants of the rural county did not rejoice at our misfortune. Instead, they became incensed. As they learned more about the crime, the sheer callousness of it outraged their beliefs of right and wrong, outraged the deeply ingrained chivalry integral to country folk, and suddenly, Alex and I and the peregrines (which astounded me) became a rallying point. The local Presbyterian minister mentioned the falcons in his Sunday sermon; after the service came a stream of offers for the loan of camping gear. People approached Alex and me on the streets and in the grocery store and asked if they could assist us. I was moved by their concern, especially considering that, in effect, these people could be abandoning what they had perceived as their own interest, what they had hoped to gain from development, by reaching a hand to help us. As for our supporters—Edna, Pat Waters, the sheriff, among others—they became doubly protective and volunteered any necessity to complete our study.

I feared it wouldn't last—emotions can't sustain running at high pitch—but I reminded myself that it was an important opening of the fragile doors of communication with the local community. I welcomed the chance to talk with someone— farmer, rancher, shop owner—to chat without hostility about the peregrines and the future of the mountain. Some, of course, remained unconvinced, but others began to adjust their opinions, throwing light on a subject that previously had received little. Perhaps this had to happen, perhaps the beginning of all progress must start with a catharsis, a breaking down of prejudices.

Mr. Fitch's reaction was the most surprising. After recovering from the shock of the trailer, he became angered over the hostile threat to us, and the falcons, which he began referring to as "his charge." He and Barry both worried over Alex's and my stubborn determination to return to Chimney Rock to see the nesting season through, but they at last acquiesced, realizing it was no use to argue.

For me, coming back to a place that had been torn apart by hatred left an unhealable rift in the trust I had ascribed to it, no matter how hard I persuaded myself that it was still the same place. A sense of security was gone; there was a new awareness of the fragility of life, and its tenuousness. The birds were unchanged, but the way I saw them wasn't. The romantic gleam that had led me to become a wildlife biologist was replaced by the deadly seriousness of the game. I learned one can't be "relativistic" and be a dedicated scientist; one has to know her beliefs and why she believes in them, and then one has to be willing to stand for them, in fairness and integrity, even when their foundation is shaken—especially when their foundation is shaken.

In the long, quiet hours of late September, I went over and over again in my mind the accusations and the bitterness that led up to the vandalism on Chimney Rock. Much of what the contractors, the foresters, the businessmen, and the political leaders of the community said they wanted was understandable and reasonable. They wished to make money on the resources that the peregrines were apparently locking up. The falcons were the stumbling block; without the falcons there would be no problem. The debate was between economic viability and the environment, and the two were mutually exclusive.

But were they really?

I watched Arthur flying free, careening through the sky on a ferris wheel of kinetic energy. A bird, a mere bird, but I thought again about what he has given man:

The peregrine falcon has given us time—time to find out about the dangers of toxic pesticides before they had the chance to unleash their detrimental effects on us. The falcons are valuable to man because they occupy the same position in the food chain ladder as we do. We are both at the top, both predators. By carefully examining the effect of pesticides on birds of prey, we have been spared a miserable fate, for the chemicals that have harmed them potentially could produce like reactions in us. They are a barometer for man, an indicator of the health of our environment.

But I could hear the rebuttal: there are other predators besides peregrines. Let the peregrines be sacrificed. Other species can do the same thing.

Was that true?

It is indisputable that each living species is a holding tank for unique genetic material that has evolved over thousands of years. This information cannot be copied or retrieved if it's destroyed. Therefore, no matter how unimportant a species might seem, it may someday be of incomparable value to all of us.

Of course, I have heard the response to this argument many times already: "Yes, just like the snail darter. The 'invaluable' snail darter. What a necessary little creature. So valuable that it shuts down a billion dollar dam project. Or the spotted owl in Oregon, forcing the timber industry into oblivion."

For so many people, the Endangered Species Act boils down to the apparent foolishness of stopping economic development for the safekeeping of a silly, inconsequential animal like the snail darter or spotted owl or peregrine falcon. But this view is actually the shortsighted one. We forget that it is from a "silly, inconsequential" animal indeed, a lowly fungus, that man was given penicillin.

Each year, one quarter of all prescriptions written in the United States contain chemicals that have been discovered in plants and animals. The names are familiar: penicillin, chloromycin, streptomycin, tetracycline, and others. Simple but obscure species have given us breakthroughs for treating scores of deadly illnesses: bubonic plague, tuberculosis, typhoid fever, diphtheria, scarlet fever, syphilis, bacterial pneumonia. A drug prepared from a little known flower discovered in a tropical forest, the rosy periwinkle, has now given a child that suffers from leukemia four chances in five to survive.

Where would man be today if we unwittingly had destroyed these plants and animals before their chemistries had been discovered? Isn't preserving life part of economic development? It seemed so to me.

I was aware that scientists had recently discovered that snails and mollusks didn't contract cancer. This single, modest item has now incited a quest to discover the chemicals that might be causing this amazing immunity. So even snails had a purpose—humble snails that might potentially be holding within them the answer to the prevention of cancer in man.

Albert was preening on a ledge after having finished a royal repast of a Steller's jay. With liquid movements, he scratched his fully extended wing with his powerful talon. His balance was superb. After one wing was done, he proceeded onto the other. Then he scratched his head and shook himself. Like a typical California sun worshiper, Albert leaned forward to catch the lowering, lingering rays of the late afternoon sun. His belly full, he was soon asleep, the golden sun dancing on his feathers. He was blissfully unaware that such moments of facile living would come more rarely now.

Taking off my sweater to enjoy the same effect, it came to me how easy it is to believe that short-term benefits last forever. How simple, when things are going well, to become too self-satisfied in our accomplishments. Revelling in instant gratification makes us forget that such things don't stay the same for long. Change inevitably comes; how we respond to it depends on how well prepared we are.

As a scientist, I knew that the search for new drugs to prevent diseases could not stop. To pause, basking in our accomplishments, even for a minute was a deadly mistake, for bacteria become resistant to antibiotics over time; this being so, we are continually in a race against time to find substitutes for the antibiotics we now depend upon.

To count on current drugs to always work is a fool's dream. To stay ahead, we must study the chemistries of more species, but first, we must save the species.

Saving species presents another problem, one that the peregrines of Chimney Rock crystallized for me. If a species like the peregrine is endangered, should we put it in a zoo to protect it, thus freeing up tracts of land for development?

Zoos are marvelous places for captive breeding and for species research. Yet there is a snag. A species will always be intricately entwined with its natural condition.

Again the axiomatic proverb of biology came to mind: a species is its habitat, pure and simple. Species protection can never be separated from habitat protection. Like a leading part in a play, an animal or plant plays a principal role in its ecosystem; you can't remove it and expect the play to go on like it did before. The roles are all changed, the meaning lost, the ending altered.

One of the most urgent problems we have in the world today is the destruction of natural habitat, which results from industrial, residential, and recreational development. To a certain degree, this is inevitable and entirely justifiable. But a point of no return comes when man starts destroying species that he needs to insure genetic diversity.

Each species, with its unique function and chemistry, is like a single volume housed in a gigantic library, the greatest reference library of all, the natural ecosystem. If our goal is to protect the volumes and volumes of information that benefit all of us, now and in the future, then we must be certain to insure the integrity of the natural ecosystem.

That was the foundation of the Endangered Species Act: protecting species—all the species we can—that are on the brink of extinction, in order to restore their populations so that once again they are self-supporting, working parts of their ecosystem. Often the task is unrelenting, discouraging, and, as I know first hand now, greatly misunderstood. People are generally under the impression that protecting a species results in keeping critical resources from people. In fact, it is just the opposite. The basis of preserving endangered species is to keep critical resources for people.

In addition to their medical benefits, wild species hold keys to unlock today's unanswerables in agriculture. The productivity of our major crops cannot be sustained at present levels, or increased, unless there is a continual inpouring of new genetic variety. The majority of this influx comes from wild plants.

Modern industry is also dependent on plant and animal species. Today, the sources of many chemicals we rely upon, compounds that are used as stabilizers and emulsifiers in hundreds of products—plastics, deodorants, detergents, paints, paper products, coolants, lubricating oils and waxes, to name a few—have come from originally wild species.

The cogent fact is a simple one. As Einstein expounded, most scientific principles are simple. Once an animal or plant species is obliterated by man, its chemistry, too, is gone forever. Extinction means that we humans have reduced the gene pool or, in other words, thrown the library volumes away without knowing what they contained. And once we have disposed of them, it is impossible to retrieve them.

Arthur was a simple bird, but he held so much within. And, as I learned from living with him, his intrinsic value, like that of all life, existed independent of and exceeded his useful and practical value to mankind. There was so much of the peregrine that was unknown, waiting to be discovered, or obliterated, by man.

Chapter Twenty-Six

 SOMETIME DURING the first week of October, Bold Leopold, always the first to take initiative in everything, left Chimney Rock to begin his long and arduous winter migration. Where he would reside was open to speculation; much is unknown about peregrine wintering habits. The only certainty was that he would seek someplace with relatively stable prey populations, either the southwestern United States, Central America, or northern South America. The last two areas were potentially dangerous spots where he could pick up further organochlorine pesticide contamination from croplands. His departure was not cut and dried, rather it happened gradually over a period of days, as he continued to spend more and more time, even nights, away from home. And then, Alex and I just did not see him anymore, and the separation at last was complete.

I always wondered how Albert, who apparently had no intention of budging out on his own, felt about Leopold's desertion. Perhaps it did not affect him. But in the evenings as he perched close to home, he seemed to be waiting for something, either Leopold or food, probably food. Albert was developing well as a hunter now. He was prepared to begin his solo excursion anytime, but I think he still hoped that Arthur might forget and drop off a tasty morsel now and then, which Arthur on occasion did.

The two peregrines had little interaction during the day, though at night they roosted near each other on separate ledges fifty feet apart. I suspect Albert was secretly comforted by Arthur's presence, whereas Arthur resignedly "put up" with his late bloomer. There was no sign of discontent or power struggle between them, even though I watched for it closely, aware of the theory some ornithologists hold that parent peregrines will, when the time is right, drive their young from the cliff to force them out on their own. Arthur never attempted to push either youngster from the home territory, and I decided his was more of the Dr. Spock approach. Relaxed and gentle-handed in his parenting, he was content to let nature take its course where it applied to Albert. Eventually Albert would have to leave home, either by his own volition or when the reduction of the food supply forcibly dictated it.

Arthur's heavy task of raising and schooling his offspring was now alleviated, and during the scant bit of free time between the close of the breeding season and the onset of winter, he rested. Once again he spent long hours at his cliff. He looked worn-out and bedraggled, but this was not from the beating he took as a single parent but from the process of annual molting. He had lost several of his long, tapered primary feathers and looked the part of a soldier wounded in action; but in eighteen to twenty-six weeks, by spring and in time for courtship, the molt would be completed, and he would be regally clothed in handsome new feathers, ready to begin another nesting season, if a new mate could be found.

A family of coyotes was sending up its choral message to the evening wind as I slowly walked down the mountainside that had been my home for the last four and a half months. As I passed a gnarled and furrowed Gambel oak, the deeply lobed leaves rustled in the wind. I was reminded of the shy rock wren who always ran along the cliff to take cover in its shade. I missed its happy music rising up from the rocks; its song always touched me like a reunion with a well-loved friend.

The barren, sandstone face of Chimney Rock was washed russet by the mid-October sunset, and somewhere sleeping for the night in the security of a sequestered ledge were Albert and Arthur, who would stay there until the dawn. Perhaps it was because it was my last night at the cliff, but somehow I was spellbound by the sound of autumn crickets and by the purity of the moment, a frozen bit of eternity where suddenly you can see backwards and forwards into the timeless heart of things. The flowers, the rocks, the trees, and my own soul were unexpectedly lucid, and my motivation to save the peregrines became perfectly clear.

I cherished what the peregrine represented, what the thought and sight of the falcons did to my spirit. Like whooping cranes or California condors or brown pelicans or even the most fragile, endangered penstamen, the peregrine was God's creature. By understanding its beauty and function, I appreciated, more and more, my own Creator. It boiled down to this one thing: if the peregrine was living free, then I too was free. If it was sacrificed to progress, then something in my spirit was sacrificed.

The large ceremonial kiva crowning the top of the mountain caught the sun's last reflection as it tipped over the rolling San Juan River Valley. I thought again of the ancient Indians who had roamed this wild country for hundreds of years: the basketmakers weaving their fine baskets and the Pueblo Anasazis creating with their masonry marvels of architecture.

The once powerful Anasazis had now disappeared. Would peregrine falcons soon be forced to meet a similar fate? Arthur,

Jenny, Bold Leopold, and Albert were what gave the land its life. With their demise, I could foresee the spirit that gave life to the canyons, cliffs, and mountains becoming a faded memory. Memories can be treasured, even sustained for long years, but their power is disembodied; they can only hint of a land that was. That was not enough for future generations.

I had made my decision. The study must continue. I would come back in six months for another spring and summer and fall, longer than that if necessary, to continue with the research I had begun and see it through, whatever the risks involved. Mrs. Fawcett was right; I was prepared now. The novice scientist at last had fledged, and a stronger, more assured woman had emerged, honed by a mountain and four wild peregrine falcons.

In the distance I heard Arthur's cry. As long as Arthur lived and his cliff remained undisturbed, he would return in early spring to the place that had claimed him, for the male peregrine's love of his cliff is the strongest bond in his life, even greater than his attachment to his mate.

My steps lightened, quickened, as the blue-bunch wheatgrass hissed between my ankles. As long as Arthur and his offspring freely sailed on the wing, I knew there would always be hope.

Epilogue

THE FOLLOWING SPRING, I returned to Chimney Rock, and stayed to study the peregrines for three more years. I continued working with Alex, Mr. Fitch, Pat Waters, Barry Layne, and John, the young French Canadian engineer (whom I happily ended up marrying, but that is another story) all the months I lived in the wild San Juan Mountains. My first spring back, Arthur came home to the eyrie after his long winter and was fortunate to attract a new mate, a yearling female we named "Lady," who remained with him for five subsequent nesting seasons. Alex and I continued and expanded our research, using more sophisticated equipment to conduct radio telemetry experiments and delving into new recovery methods, including captive breeding and cross-fostering of nestling peregrines. Over this time, I watched with increasing amazement as people from nearby rural communities continued to grow in their acceptance of the peregrines, with a sizeable number beginning to take actual pride in the birds. Some, in fact became ardent advocates, including one Mr. Preston Fitch.

The peregrine falcon recovery program of North America is generally believed to be one of the most positive and far-sighted wildlife conservation endeavors ever attempted. Since 1974, hundreds of captive-bred and -raised peregrine falcons have been returned, or hacked, to the wild, with several success stories being reported as early as 1979. With the reduction of organocholorine-residue contamination in the environment, the productivity of wild peregrines is increasing in the United States, though in other parts of the world its future is not as certain.

Problems still remain, however. As has been documented over and over again, no species of wildlife can be thought of as safe from extermination; man's growing dominance throughout the globe continues to affect all that remains of what is natural and wild. The problems of places like Chimney Rock will not go away, even if for a time they simmer quietly. Pressure for limited resources is increasing everywhere. For the peregrine and other wild species, our hope lies in our continual expansion of knowledge woven together with new methods of creative management and in unceasing, vigilant support of important legislation.

I have been away from Chimney Rock for six years. Two years after I left, Arthur and Lady did not return to Chimney Rock. Since then, the eyrie has remained uninhabited. Today, the mountain on which I lived still stands in its undeveloped state, waiting. For what? For a large-scale tourist attraction or for the chance a peregrine might one day return to this first-class cliff that has been used by peregrines for hundreds of years?

The verdict is still not in.

Last April, however, two new peregrine researchers stopped by for a brief sojourn at Chimney Rock. They reported seeing a lone bird, a peregrine, circling high above the mountain. The bird did not light, but came back three times, apparently trying to make up its mind. Scientists believe it may yet decide to nest on Chimney Rock.

I like to believe it might be Albert.